Henry John Stephen

A Handbook of the Law Relating to the Management of Parliamentary, Municipal and County Council Elections

Henry John Stephen

A Handbook of the Law Relating to the Management of Parliamentary, Municipal and County Council Elections

ISBN/EAN: 9783337154547

Printed in Europe, USA, Canada, Australia, Japan

Cover: Foto ©Suzi / pixelio.de

More available books at **www.hansebooks.com**

A HANDBOOK

OF THE

LAW RELATING TO THE MANAGEMENT

OF

PARLIAMENTARY, MUNICIPAL AND COUNTY COUNCIL ELECTIONS,

SECOND EDITION,

BY

HENRY STEPHEN, Esquire,

OF THE MIDDLE TEMPLE, BARRISTER-AT-LAW,

Editor of 9th Edition Stephen's Commentaries and Joint Author of the County Council Compendium.

LONDON:

WATERLOW AND SONS LIMITED, LONDON WALL.

1888.

PREFACE.

THIS handy book is designed for persons who may require, in a compendious form and for immediate use, a brief statement of the Law relating to the machinery of Elections. The Ballot Act, 1872, and those portions of the Local Government Act, 1888, and the Municipal Corporations Act, 1882, which refer to the conduct of Elections are printed in an annotated form; a chapter showing the effect of breaches of the provisions of the Acts upon all Election and a Table of References to the Statutes which prescribe the procedure at Parliamentary, Municipal and County Council Elections being added, with the view of enabling everyone to ascertain what the law is, and where it may be found.

HENRY STEPHEN.

1, MITRE COURT BUILDINGS,
    TEMPLE.

PARLIAMENTARY, MUNICIPAL AND COUNTY COUNCIL ELECTIONS.

The Law relating to Procedure at Parliamentary, Municipal and County Council elections is contained in the Ballot Act, 1872, the Municipal Corporations Act, 1882, the Local Government Act, 1888, and the Corrupt Practices Acts of 1883 and 1884.

With regard to the nomination of candidates at parliamentary elections the Ballot Act (35 & 36 Vict. c. 33) enacts that :—

WHEREAS it is expedient to amend the law relating to procedure at parliamentary and municipal elections :

Be it enacted by the Queen's most Excellent Majesty, by and with the advice and consent of the Lords Spiritual and Temporal, and Commons, in this present Parliament assembled, and by the authority of the same, as follows :—

1. A candidate for election to serve in parliament for a county or borough shall be nominated in writing. The writing shall be subscribed by two registered electors of such county or borough as proposer and seconder, and by eight other registered electors of the same county or borough as assenting to the nomination, and shall be delivered during the time appointed for the election to the returning officer by the candidate himself, or his proposer or seconder.

Nomination of candidates for parliamentary elections.

If at the expiration of one hour after the time appointed for the election no more candidates stand nominated than there are vacancies to be filled up, the returning officer shall forthwith declare the

1

candidates who may stand nominated to be elected, and return their names to the Clerk of the Crown in Chancery ; but if at the expiration of such hour more candidates stand nominated than there are vacancies to be filled up, the returning officer shall adjourn the election and shall take a poll in manner in this Act mentioned.

A candidate may, during the time appointed for the election, but not afterwards, withdraw from his candidature by giving a notice to that effect, signed by him, to the returning officer ; Provided that the proposer of a candidate nominated in his absence out of the United Kingdom may withdraw such candidate by a written notice signed by him and delivered to the returning officer, together with a written declaration of such absence of the candidate.

If after the adjournment of an election by the returning officer for the purpose of taking a poll one of the candidates nominated shall die before the poll has commenced, the returning officer shall, upon being satisfied of the fact of such death, countermand notice of the poll, and all the proceedings with reference to the election shall be commenced afresh in all respects as if the writ had been received by the returning officer on the day on which proof was given to him of such death : Provided that no fresh nomination shall be necessary in the case of a candidate who stood nominated at the time of the countermand of the poll.

For the nomination of candidates at Municipal and County Council elections reference must be made to the Municipal Corporations Act, 1882 (45 & 46 Vict. c. 50), and the Local Government Act, 1888 (51 & 52 Vict. c. 41). The former of these Acts enacts :—

Nomination of candidates at municipal and county council elections.

53. At an election of councillors for a whole borough the returning officer shall be the mayor.

(2.) At an election for a ward the returning officer shall be the alderman assigned for that purpose by the council at the meeting of the 9th of November.

54. Nine days at least before the day for the election of a councillor, the town clerk shall prepare

and sign a notice thereof and publish it by fixing it on the town hall, and, in the case of a ward election, in some conspicuous place in the ward.

55. The nomination of candidates for the office of councillor shall be conducted in accordance with the rules in Part II. of the Third Schedule.

56. (1.) If the number of valid nominations exceeds that of the vacancies, the councillors shall be elected from among the persons nominated.

(2.) If the number of valid nominations is the same as that of the vacancies, the persons nominated shall be deemed to be elected.

(3.) If the number of valid nominations is less than that of the vacancies, the persons nominated shall be deemed to be elected, and such of the retiring councillors for the borough or ward as were highest on the poll at their election, or, if the poll was equal, or there was no poll, as are selected for that purpose by the mayor, shall be deemed to be re-elected to make up the required number.

(4.) If there is no valid nomination, the retiring councillors shall be deemed to be re-elected.

57. If an election of councillors is not contested, the returning officer shall publish a list of the persons elected not later than eleven o'clock in the morning on the day of election.

Rules as to Nomination in Elections of Councillors.

1. Every candidate for the office of councillor, must be nominated in writing.

2. The writing must be subscribed by two burgesses of the borough, or, in the case of a ward election, of the ward, as proposer and seconder, and by eight other burgesses of the borough or ward, as assenting to the nomination.

3. Each candidate must be nominated by a separate nomination paper, but the same burgesses, or any of them, may subscribe as many nomination

papers as there are vacancies to be filled, but no more.

4. Each person nominated must be enrolled in the burgess roll, or entered in the separate non-resident list required by this Act to be made.

5. The nomination paper must state the surname and other names of the candidate, with his abode and description.

6. The town clerk shall provide nomination papers, and shall supply any burgess with as many nomination papers as may be required, and shall, at the request of any burgess, fill up a nomination paper.

7. Every nomination paper subscribed as aforesaid, must be delivered by the candidate or his proposer, or seconder, at the town clerk's office, seven days at least before the day of election, and before five o'clock in the afternoon of the last day for delivery of nomination papers.

8. The town clerk shall forthwith send notice of every such nomination to each candidate.

9. The mayor shall attend at the town hall on the day next after the last day for delivery of nomination papers for a sufficient time, between the hours of two and four in the afternoon, and shall decide on the validity of every objection made in writing to a nomination paper.

10. Where a person subscribes more nomination papers than one, his subscription shall be inoperative in all but the one which is first delivered.

11. Each candidate may, by writing signed by him, or, if he is absent from the United Kingdom, then his proposer or seconder may, by writing signed by him, appoint a person (in this schedule referred as the candidate's representative) to attend the proceedings before the mayor on behalf of the candidate, and this appointment must be delivered to the town clerk before five o'clock in the afternoon of the last day for delivery of nomination papers.

12. Each candidate and his representative, but no other person, except for the purpose of assisting the mayor, shall be entitled to attend the proceedings before the mayor.

13. Each candidate and his representative may, during the time appointed for the attendance of the mayor for the purposes of this schedule, object to the nomination paper of any other candidate for the borough or ward.

14. The decision of the mayor shall be given in writing, and shall, if disallowing an objection, be final, but if allowing an objection, shall be subject to reversal on petition questioning the election return.

15. The town clerk shall, at least four days before the day of election, cause the surnames and other names of all persons validly nominated, with their respective abodes and descriptions, and the names of the persons subscribing their nomination papers as proposers and seconders, to be printed and fixed on the town hall, and in the case of a ward election, in some conspicuous place in the ward.

16. The nomination of a person absent from the United Kingdom shall be void, unless his written consent given within one month before the day of his nomination in the presence of his witnesses is produced at the time of his nomination.

17. Where the number of valid nominations exceeds that of the vacancies, any candidate may withdraw from his candidature by notice signed by him, and delivered at the town clerk's office not later than two o'clock in the afternoon of the day next after the last day for delivery of nomination papers : Provided that such notices shall take effect in the order in which they are delivered, and that no such notice shall have effect so as to reduce the number of candidates ultimately standing nominated below the number of vacancies.

18. In and for the purposes of the provisions of this Act relating to proceedings preliminary to election, the burgess roll or ward roll, and a person whose name is inserted in one of the lists from which the burgess roll or ward roll will be made up, shall be deemed to be enrolled in that roll although that roll is not yet completed.

And these sections and schedule have been adopted by the latter of the statutes mentioned above with certain modifica-

tions contained in the 75th section, which provides in sub-
sections:

(4.) A reference in this Act, or in the enactments
applied by this Act to the returning officer or
to the mayor or to the alderman shall, so far
as relates to the election of any such councillor, be construed to refer to the returning
officer, and any such deputy as above mentioned.

(5.) A reference in the said enactments to the
town clerk so far as respects the election of
any such councillor shall be construed to
refer to the returning officer or his deputy,
and as respects matters subsequent to the
election shall be construed to refer to the
clerk of the county council.

(6.) In a borough the returning officer for the
purpose of the election of councillors of the
borough shall continue to be the same as
heretofore, and where an electoral division of
the county is co-extensive with or wholly
comprised in such borough, shall at the
election in such division of a councillor of
the county council act as the returning
officer in pursuance of a writ directed to
him from the county returning officer,
and so far as respects that election shall
follow the instructions of, and return the
names of the persons elected to the county
returning officer in like manner as if he were
a deputy returning officer, and any decision
of an objection shall be subject to revision
by the county returning officer accordingly,
and a reference in the said enactments to the
town clerk shall, as respects the borough, be
construed to refer to the town clerk.

(7.) Some place fixed by the returning officer
shall, except where the election is in a
borough, be substituted for the town clerk's
office, and, as respects the hearing of objections to nomination papers, for the town
hall, but such place shall, if the electoral

division is the whole or part of an urban district, be in that district, and in any other case shall be in the electoral division or in an adjoining electoral division.

(8.) The returning officer shall forthwith, after the election of county councillors for the county, return the names of the persons elected to the clerk of the county council.

(9.) The period between the nomination and election may be such period, not exceeding six days, as the returning officer may fix.

The following cases on the construction of these sections are useful: MATHER *v.* BROWN, L.R. 1, C.P.D. 596, 45 L.J. Q.B. 547, and HENRY *v.* ARMITAGE L.R. 12 Q.B.D. 257, 53 L.J. Q.B. 111, which relate to the filling up of nomination papers as to *name*; SOPER *v.* MAYOR OF BASINGSTOKE, L.R. 2 C.P.D. 440, 46 L.J. C.P. 422 as to the *abode* of candidate. As to the power of the returning officer to decide objections: HOWES *v.* TURNER 1 C.P.D. 670, 45 L.J. Q.B. 550; MONKS *v.* JACKSON, 1 C.D. 683, 46 L.J. Q.B. 162, in which cases it was held that the returning officer could only decide whether the form of the paper was correct, and not whether it was delivered early enough.

At contested parliamentary elections the second section of the Ballot Act enacts that:—

2. In the case of a poll at an election the votes shall be given by ballot. The ballot of each voter shall consist of a paper (in this Act called a ballot paper) showing the names and description of the candidates. Each ballot paper shall have a number printed on the back, and shall have attached a counterfoil with the same number printed on the face. At the time of voting the ballot paper shall be marked on both sides with an official mark, and delivered to the voter within the polling station, and the number of such voter on the register of voters shall be marked on the counterfoil (*a*), and

Poll at elections.

(*a.*) The question was raised, but not decided, in PICKERING *v.* STARTIN, 28 L. T. 111, whether the failure of the returning officer to mark on the counterfoils of twenty-nine of the voting papers the number of the voter appearing on the burgess roll would avoid the election. It is submitted such an irregularity would not have that effect. See pp. 62-65.

the voter having secretly marked his vote on the paper, and folded it up so as to conceal his vote shall place it in a closed box in the presence of the officer presiding at the polling station (in this Act called "the presiding officer") after having shown to him the official mark at the back.

Any ballot paper which has not on its back the official mark, or on which votes are given to more candidates than the voter is entitled to vote for, or on which anything, except the said number on the back, is written or marked by which the voter can be identified, shall be void, and not counted (a).

After the close of the poll the ballot boxes shall be sealed up, so as to prevent the introduction of additional ballot papers, and shall be taken charge of by the returning officer, and that officer shall, in the presence of such agents, if any, of the candidates as may be in attendance, open the ballot boxes, and ascertain the result of the poll by counting the votes given to each candidate, and shall forthwith declare to be elected the candidates or candidate to whom the majority of votes have been given, and return their names to the Clerk of the Crown in Chancery. The decision of the returning officer as to any question arising in respect of any ballot paper shall be final, subject to reversal on petition questioning the election or return.

Where an equality of votes is found to exist between any candidates at an election for a county or borough, and the addition of a vote would entitle any of such candidates to be declared elected, the returning officer, if a registered elector of such county or borough, may give such additional vote, but shall not in any other case be entitled to vote at an election for which he is returning officer.

And this section is, by the fifty-eighth section of the Municipal Corporations Act and the seventy-fifth section of the Local Government Act, applied to contested municipal

---

(a.) The cases bearing upon the rejection of ballot papers for informalities, &c., are collected at pp. 62-65.

and county council elections. The former of these sections is as under :—

(1.) If an election of councillors is contested, the poll shall, as far as circumstances admit, be conducted as the poll at a contested parliamentary election is by the Ballot Act, 1872, directed to be conducted, and subject to the modifications expressed in Part III. of the Third Schedule, and to the other provisions of this Act the provisions of the Ballot Act, 1872, relating to a poll at a parliamentary election (including the provisions relating to the duties of the returning officer after the close of the poll), shall apply to a poll of an election of councillors.

(2.) Every person entitled to vote may vote for any number of candidates not exceeding the number of vacancies.

(3.) The poll shall commence at eight o'clock in the forenoon and close at eight o'clock in the afternoon of the same day (48 Vict. c. 10).

(4.) But if one hour elapses during which no vote is tendered, and the returning officer has not received notice that any person has within that hour been prevented from coming to the poll by any riot, violence, or other unlawful means, the returning officer may, if he thinks fit, close the poll at any time before eight o'clock (48 Vict. c. 10).

(5.) Where an equality of votes is found to exist between any candidates, and the addition of a vote would entitle any of those candidates to be declared elected, the returning officer, whether entitled or not to vote in the first instance, may give such additional vote by word of mouth or in writing.

(6.) Nothing in the Ballot Act, 1872, as applied by this Act shall be deemed to authorise the appointment of any agents of a candidate at a municipal election, but if in the case of a municipal election, an agent of a candidate is appointed, and notice in writing of the appointment is given to the returning officer one clear day before the polling day, then the provisions of the Ballot Act, 1872, with respect to agents of candidates, shall as far as regards that agent, apply in the case of that election.

With regard to offences at *all* elections the Ballot Act provides that :—

Offences in respect of nomination papers, ballot papers, and ballot boxes.

3. Every person who—

(1.) Forges or fraudulently defaces or fraudulently destroys any nomination paper, or delivers to the returning officer any nomination paper, knowing the same to be forged ; or

(2.) Forges or counterfeits or fraudulently defaces or fraudulently destroys any ballot paper or the official mark on any ballot paper ; or

(3.) Without due authority supplies any ballot paper to any person ; or

(4.) Fraudulently puts into any ballot box any paper other than the ballot paper which he is authorised by law to put in ; or

(5.) Fraudulently takes out of the polling station any ballot paper ; or

(6.) Without due authority destroys, takes, opens, or otherwise interferes with any ballot box or packet of ballot papers then in use for the purposes of the election ;

shall be guilty of a misdemeanor, and be liable, if he is a returning officer or an officer or clerk in attendance at a polling station to imprisonment for any term not exceeding two years, with or without hard labour, and if he is any other person, to imprisonment for any term not exceeding six months with or without hard labour.

Any attempt to commit any offence specified in this section shall be punishable in the manner in which the offence itself is punishable.

In any indictment or other prosecution for an offence in relation to the nomination papers, ballot boxes, ballot papers, and marking instruments at an election, the property in such papers, boxes, and instruments may be stated to be in the returning officer at such election, as well as the property in the counterfoils.

In REG. *v.* BEARDSALL (1 Q. B. D. 452), a deputy returning officer at a municipal election was convicted of an offence under this section. The court decided in that case that production of ballot papers, &c., can be ordered by a County Court Judge under Rule 64 of Part II., Schedule I. of the Act, in aid of a prosecution for an offence against the Ballot Act.

4. Every officer, clerk, and agent in attendance at a polling station shall maintain and aid in maintaining the secrecy of the voting of such station, and shall not communicate, except for some purpose authorised by law, before the poll is closed, to any person any information as to the name or number on the register of voters of any elector who has or has not applied for a ballot paper or voted at that station *(a)*, or as to the official mark, and no such officer, clerk, or agent, and no person whosoever, shall interfere with or attempt to interfere with a voter when marking his vote, or otherwise attempt to obtain in the polling station information as to the candidate for whom any voter in such station is about to vote or has voted, or communicate at any time to any person any information obtained in a

Infringement of secrecy.

(*a.*) In order to justify a conviction under this part of the section, it must be shown that the information reached the mind of the person to whom it is communicated, and it is not enough to show that such person had the means of knowing it. Therefore, where the evidence was that the personation agent had gone from the polling station to the committee room of the candidate for whom he was agent, and had there left his part of the burgess roll, on which he had put a mark against the name of every voter who had obtained a ballot paper, but did not show that any one there had looked into such part of the burgess roll, or had in fact obtained any information from it, the court held that there was no evidence on which a magistrate ought to convict the agent. STANNANOUGHT *v.* HAZELDINE, 4 C. P. Div. 191; 48 L. J. M. C. 89; 40 L. T. 589.

polling station as to the candidate for whom any voter in such station is about to vote or has voted (*a*), or as to the number on the back of the ballot paper given to any voter at such station. Every officer, clerk, and agent in attendance at the counting of the votes shall maintain and aid in maintaining the secrecy of the voting, and shall not attempt to ascertain at such counting the number on the back of any ballot paper, or communicate any information obtained at such counting as to the candidate for whom any vote is given in any particular ballot paper. No person shall directly or indirectly induce any voter to display his ballot paper after he shall have marked the same, so as to make known to any person the name of the candidate for or against whom he has so marked his vote.

Every person who acts in contravention of the provisions of this section shall be liable, on summary conviction before two justices of the peace, to imprisonment for any term not exceeding six months, with or without hard labour.

5. [The first paragraph of this section is repealed by the Corrupt and Illegal Practices Act, 1883 (the 46 & 47 Vict., c. 51), 5th schedule (*b*). The remaining paragraphs are not affected and are as follows] :—

The local authority (as hereinafter defined) of

(*a*.) Upon a charge of violating the secrecy of the ballot by telling how an illiterate voter had voted, the information communicated by the accused is, of itself, sufficient evidence to convict him of the offence. Reg. *v.* Unkles, 8 Ir. R., C. L. 50.

(*b*.) The 47th section of the Corrupt Practices Act, 1883, which is practically in substitution of the repealed portion of the above section, applies to *England* and *Wales* only, and provides that in a county, so far as is reasonably practicable, every elector shall have a polling place within a distance of three miles from his residence, and that in a borough every elector shall have a polling place within one mile of his residence.

The provisions of the 5th section of the Ballot Act (*supra*) and of the 47th section of the Corrupt Practices Act, 1883, do not apply to Scotland or Ireland.

every borough shall take into consideration the
division of such borough into polling districts, and,
if they think it desirable, by order, divide such
borough into polling districts in such manner as
they may think most convenient for taking the
votes of the electors at a poll.

The local authority of every county and borough
shall, on or before the first day of May, One thousand
eight hundred and seventy-three, send to one of
Her Majesty's Principal Secretaries of State, to be
laid by him before both Houses of Parliament, a
copy of any order made by such authority in pursuance of this section, and a report, in such form as
he may require, stating how far the provisions of
this Act with respect to polling districts have been
complied with in their county or borough ; and if
they make any order after the first day of May, One
thousand eight hundred and seventy-three, with
respect to polling districts or polling places in their
county or borough, they shall send a copy of such
order to the said Secretary of State, to be laid by
him before both Houses of Parliament.

The local authority of a county or borough in this
section means the authority having power to divide
such county or borough into polling districts under
section thirty-four of the Representation of the
People Act, 1867, and any enactments amending
that section ; and such authority shall exercise the
powers thereby given to them for the purposes of
this section ; and the provisions of the said section
as to the local authority of a borough constituted by
the combination of two or more municipal boroughs
shall apply to a borough constituted by the combination of a municipal borough and other places,
whether municipal boroughs or not ; and in the case
of a borough of which a town council is not the
local authority, and which is not wholly situate
within one petty sessional division, the justices of
the peace for the county in which such borough or
the larger part thereof in area is situate, assembled
at some court of general or quarter sessions, or at
some adjournment thereof, shall be the local

authority thereof, and shall for this purpose have jurisdiction over the whole of such borough ; and in the case of such borough and of a county, a court of general sessions shall be assembled within twenty-one days after the passing of this Act, and any such court may be assembled and adjourned from time to time for the purpose.

No election shall be questioned by reason of any non-compliance with this section or any informality relative to polling districts or polling places, and any order made by a local authority in relation to polling districts or polling places shall apply only to lists of voters made subsequently to its date, and to registers of voters formed out of such lists, and to elections held after the time at which a register of voters so formed has come into force : Provided that where any such order is made between the first day of July and the first day of November in any year, and does not create any new division between two or more polling districts of any parish for which a separate poor rate is or can be made, such order shall apply to the register of voters which comes into force next after such order is made, and to elections held after that register so comes into force; and the clerk of the peace or town clerk, as the case may be, shall copy, print and arrange the list of voters for the purpose of such register in accordance with such order.

Use of school and public room for poll at parliamentary and county council elections. 6. The returning officer at a parliamentary election may use, free of charge, for the purpose of taking the poll at such election, any room in a school receiving a grant out of moneys provided by parliament, and any room the expense of maintaining which is payable out of any local rate, but he shall make good any damage done to such room, and defray any expense incurred by the person or body of persons, corporate or unincorporate, having control over the same on account of its being used for the purpose of taking the poll as aforesaid.

The use of any room in an unoccupied house for the purpose of taking the poll shall not render any person liable to be rated or to pay any rate for such house.

This section has no application to municipal, although it has to county council elections. By section 69 of the Municipal Corporations Act, 1882, "a municipal election shall not be held in any church, chapel, or other place of public worship."

7. At any election for a county or borough, a person shall not be entitled to vote unless his name is on the register of voters for the time being in force for such county or borough, and every person whose name is on such register shall be entitled to demand and receive a ballot paper and to vote: Provided that nothing in this section shall entitle any person to vote who is prohibited from voting by any statute, or by the common law of parliament, or relieve such person from any penalties to which he may be liable for voting.

Conclusive-ness of register of voters.

This section in the case of parliamentary elections makes the register conclusive, *for the purposes of the poll,* of the right of the person named therein to vote. The same result is attained with regard to municipal and county council elections by 45 & 46 Vict. c. 50, s. 51, and 51 and 52 Vict. c. 41, s. 75. It is apprehended that the intention of the provision is *not* that any objection of the kind mentioned therein may be taken in the polling booth, but to ensure that the enacting part should not be held to restore or make absolute the qualification of a man who had no qualification at all. "Nothing shall take place at the polling booth but a reference to the register to ascertain whether the person who presents himself is the person upon the register or not."— Lush, J., in the WORCESTER CASE 3 O'M. & H. 186. A vote which has been given may, however, *on a scrutiny,* be challenged on the ground that the voter comes within the proviso and is a person prohibited from voting (see STOWE v. JOLLIFFE, 43 L. J., C. P. 265).

Duties of Returning and Election Officers.

The Ballot Act, 1872, provides as follows:—

8. Subject to the provisions of this Act, every returning officer shall provide such nomination papers, polling stations, ballot boxes, ballot papers, stamping instruments, copies of register of voters,

General powers and duties of returning officer.

and other things, appoint and pay such officers, and
do such other acts and things as may be necessary
for effectually conducting an election in manner
provided by this Act.

All expenses properly incurred by any returning
officer in carrying into effect the provisions of this
Act, in the case of any parliamentary election, shall
be payable in the same manner as expenses incurred
in the erection of polling booths at such election are
by law payable.

Where the sheriff is returning officer for more
than one county as defined for the purposes of
parliamentary elections, he may, without prejudice
to any other power, by writing under his hand,
appoint a fit person to be his deputy for all or any
of the purposes relating to an election in any such
county, and may, by himself or such deputy, exercise
any powers and do any things which the returning
officer is authorised or required to exercise or do in
relation to such election. Every such deputy, and
also any under-sheriff, shall, in so far as he acts as
returning officer, be deemed to be included in the
term returning officer in the provisions of this Act
relating to parliamentary elections, and the enactments with which this part of this Act is to be
construed as one.

The returning officer at a municipal election is the mayor,
or if the borough be divided into wards, aldermen assigned
to that post by the council (45 & 46 Vict. c. 50, s. 67). For
a county council election, the sheriff will be the first returning officer: at future elections, he will be elected pre-
viously by the council; and if the election be in a borough
the mayor or aldermen, as the case may be, will act by virtue
of a writ directed to them by the returning officer for
the county (51 & 52 Vict. c. 41, s. 75).

The expenses of the returning officer in connection with a
parliamentary election fall in equal proportions upon the
candidates; in the case of municipal elections they are
defrayed out of the borough fund, and in county council
elections out of the county fund (51 & 52 Vict., c. 41, s. 75,
sub-s. 17).

By the 38 & 39 Vict. c. 84 (amended by 48 & 49 Vict. c. 62,
and 49 & 50 Vict. c. 57), which applies to England, Wales
and Ireland, and by the 41 & 42 Vict. c. 41, which applies to

Scotland, a returning officer is entitled to call upon the candidates to give security for an amount not exceeding the sum mentioned in the schedule within an hour of the close of the time fixed for the nomination, and any of them who fail to do so are to be declared to have withdrawn their candidature. The statute also provides for the taxation of the returning officer's charges, and the first schedule gives the maximum sums which he is entitled to charge for the various services he renders in connection with the election. If a candidate or his election agent pays a returning officer anything in excess of the maximum charges authorised by the 38 & 39 Vict. c. 84, as amended by the Acts above mentioned, he commits an illegal practice within the meaning of the Corrupt Practices Act, 1883 & 1884 (*see* the 46 & 47 Vict. c. 51, s. 8, and the 1st Schedule, Part II. 47 & 48 Vict. c. 70, s. 5, and 51 & 52 Vict. c. 41, s. 75, sub-s. 18.

9. If any person misconducts himself in the polling station, or fails to obey the lawful orders of the presiding officer, he may immediately, by order of the presiding officer, be removed from the polling station by any constable in or near that station, or any other person authorised in writing by the returning officer to remove him ; and the person so removed shall not, unless with permission of the presiding officer, again be allowed to enter the polling station during the day. *Keeping of order in station.*

Any person so removed as aforesaid, if charged with the commission in such station of any offence, may be kept in custody until he can be brought before a justice of the peace.

Provided that the powers conferred by this section shall not be exercised so as to prevent any elector who is otherwise entitled to vote at any polling station from having an opportunity of voting at such station.

10. For the purpose of the adjournment of the poll, and of every other enactment relating to the poll, a presiding officer shall have the power by law belonging to a deputy returning officer ; and any presiding officer, and any clerk appointed by the returning officer to attend at a polling station, shall have the power of asking the questions and administering the oath authorised by law to be asked of and administered to voters, and any justice of the *Powers of presiding officer and administration of oaths, &c.*

2

peace and any returning officer may take and receive any declaration authorised by this Act to be taken before him.

Municipal and county council elections.

"At an election of councillors, the presiding officer shall, if required by two burgesses or by a candidate or his agent put to any person offering to vote at the time of his presenting himself to vote, but not afterwards, the following questions or either of them: (*a*.) Are you the person enrolled in the burgess (or ward) roll now in force for this borough (or ward) as follows: (read the whole entry from the roll)? (*b*.) Have you already voted at the present election (add in case of an election for several wards, to this or any other ward)? (2.) The vote of a person required to answer either of these questions shall not be received until he has answered it. (3.) If any person wilfully makes a false answer thereto he shall be guilty of a misdemeanour. (4.) Save as by this Act authorised, no enquiry shall be permitted at an election as to the right of any person to vote." (45 & 46 Vict. c. 50, s. 59).

These questions with the necessary alterations may be asked at county council elections under 51 & 52 Vict. c. 41, s. 75.

Liability of officers for misconduct.

11. Every returning officer, presiding officer, and clerk who is guilty of any wilful misfeasance or any wilful act or omission in contravention of this Act shall, in addition to any other penalty or liability to which he may be subject, forfeit to any person aggrieved by such misfeasance, act, or omission, a penal sum not exceeding one hundred pounds.

Section fifty of the Representation of the People Act, 1867 (which relates to the acting of any returning officer, or his partner or clerk, as agent or a candidate), shall apply to any returning officer or officer appointed by him in pursuance of this Act, and to his partner or clerk.

IN PICKERING *v.* JAMES, L.R., 8 C.P. 489, the court held that the Ballot Act imposes a duty on the presiding officer at a polling station during the election to deliver to the voters voting papers bearing the official mark, and to be present during such election at the polling station, so that the voters, before depositing their voting papers in the ballot box, can shew to him the official mark on the back of such papers, and for breach of these duties an action will lie by a person who has lost his election through votes given to him being void for want of the official mark. But the court was equally divided on the question whether the Act imposed on the presiding officer, the duty of ascertaining before the voter deposited his paper in the box whether the official mark was on it or not.

12. No person who has voted at an election shall, in any legal proceeding to question the election or return, be required to state for whom he has voted. *Prohibition of disclosure of vote.*

Nor is he obliged to say to what party he belongs (The NORTH DURHAM CASE, 3 O'M. & H. 2; the HARWICH CASE ibid 64).

13. No election shall be declared invalid by reason of a non-compliance with the rules contained in the First Schedule to this Act, or any mistake in the use of the forms in the Second Schedule to this Act, if it appears to the tribunal having cognizance of the question that the election was conducted in accordance with the principles laid down in the body of this Act, and that such non-compliance or mistake did not affect the result of the election. *Non-compliance with rules.*

By 45 & 46 Vict., c. 50, s. 72, and 51 & 52 Vict. c. 41, s. 75, a similar provision is in force with regard to municipal and county council elections. The effect of these sections is discussed at pp. 62-65.

14. Where a parliamentary borough and municipal borough occupy the whole or any part of the same area, any ballot boxes or fittings for polling stations and compartments provided for such parliamentary borough or such municipal borough may be used in any municipal or parliamentary election in such borough free of charge, and any damage other than reasonable wear and tear caused to the same shall be paid as part of the expenses of the election at which they are so used. *Use of municipal ballot boxes, &c., for parliamentary election, and vice versa.*

15. This part of this Act shall, so far as is consistent with the tenor thereof, be construed as one with the enactments for the time being in force relating to the representation of the people, and to the registration of persons entitled to vote at the election of members to serve in parliament, and with any enactments otherwise relating to the subject-matter of this part of this Act, and terms used in this part *Construction of Act.*

of this Act shall have the same meaning as in the said enactments; and in construing the said enactments relating to an election or to the poll or taking the votes by poll, the mode of election and of taking the poll established by this Act shall for the purposes of the said enactments be deemed to be substituted for the mode of election or poll, or taking the votes by poll, referred to in the said enactments; and any person applying for a ballot paper under this Act shall be deemed "to tender his vote," or "to assume to vote," within the meaning of the said enactments; and any application for a ballot paper under this Act, or expression relative thereto, shall be equivalent to "voting" in the said enactments and any expressions relative thereto; and the term "polling booth" as used in the said enactments shall be deemed to include a polling station; and the term "proclamation" as used in the said enactments shall be deemed to include a public notice given in pursuance of this Act.

Alterations for application of Part I. of Ballot Act to Scotland.

16. This part of this Act shall apply to Scotland, subject to the following provisions:—

(1.) The expression "crime and offence" shall be equivalent to the expression "misdemeanor," and shall be substituted therefor:

(2.) All offences under this Act for which any person may be punished on summary conviction shall be prosecuted before the sheriff under the provisions of "The Summary Procedure Act, 1864"; and all jurisdictions, powers, and authorities necessary for that purpose are hereby conferred on sheriffs:

(3.) The expression "sheriff" shall include sheriff substitute:

(4.) The provisions of this Act relating to the division of counties and boroughs into polling districts shall not apply to Scotland:

(5.) The ballot boxes, ballot papers, stamping instruments, and other requisites for a parliamentary election shall be provided and paid for in the same manner as polling rooms or booths under the fortieth section of the Act of the second and third years of the reign of King William the Fourth, chapter sixty-five, intituled "An Act to amend the Representation of the People in Scotland"; and the reasonable remuneration of presiding officers, assistants, and clerks employed by the returning officer at such an election, and all other expenses properly incurred by the returning officer, and by sheriff clerks and town clerks, in carrying into effect the provisions of this Act, shall be paid by the candidates; provided always, that if any person shall be proposed as a candidate without his consent the person so proposing him shall be liable to defray his share of all those expenses in like manner as if he had been a candidate himself; provided also, that the fee to be paid to each presiding officer shall in no case exceed the sum of three guineas per day, and the fee to be paid to each assistant to the returning officer shall not exceed two guineas per day, and the fee to be paid to each clerk shall not exceed one guinea per day.

See the 41 & 42 Vict. c. 41, as to the right of a returning officer in Scotland to require security.

17. This part of this Act shall apply to Ireland, subject to the following modifications :— Alterations for application of Ballot Act to Ireland.

(1.) The expression "Clerk of the Crown in Chancery" shall mean the Clerk of the Crown and Hanaper in Ireland :

(2.) The preceding provisions of this part of this Act with respect to the division of counties and boroughs into polling districts shall not extend to Ireland :

(3.) In the construction of the preceding provisions of this part of this Act as applying to Ireland, section thirteen of "The Representation of the People (Ireland) Act, 1868," shall be substituted for section fifty of "The Representation of the People Act, 1867," wherever in such provisions the said last-mentioned section occurs. The provision

contained in the sixth section of this Act
providing for the use of school rooms free
of charge, for the purpose of taking the poll
at elections shall not apply to any school
adjoining or adjacent to any church or other
place of worship, nor to any school connected
with a nunnery or other religious establish-
ment :

(4.) No returning officer shall be entitled to claim,
or be paid, any sum or sums of money for
the erection of polling booths or stations and
compartments other than the sum or sums
actually and necessarily incurred and paid by
him in reference to the same, any statute or
statutes to the contrary now in force notwithstanding, nor shall the expenses of providing
sufficient polling stations or booths and compartments at every polling place exceed the
sum or sums now given and allowed by
statute in Ireland.

The 38 & 39 Vict. c. 84, regulating and controlling the
expenses of returning officers, and enabling them to require
security from the candidates, applies to Ireland.

Provisions as to polling districts and polling places in Ireland. 18. With respect to polling districts and polling
places in Ireland, the following regulations shall
have effect ; that is to say,

(1.) The Lord Lieutenant, by and with the advice
of the Privy Council in Ireland, shall appoint
special sessions to be held by the chairman of
quarter sessions and justices of the peace
having jurisdiction in each county or riding
of a county in Ireland, at such places and
times before the first day of November next
after the passing of this Act as shall seem fit
for the purpose of dividing such county or
riding into polling districts, and appointing
polling places for such districts :

(2.) The clerk of the said Privy Council shall
cause each such appointment to be notified to
the clerk of the peace of the county to

which the same relates, and shall cause notice of the same to be published twice in each of two consecutive weeks in one or more newspapers usually circulated in such county, and once in the Dublin Gazette :

(3.) The clerk of the peace of each county in Ireland shall, within five days after the receipt of such notification as aforesaid, send a written or printed notice of the same to the chairman and to every justice of the peace having jurisdiction within the county or riding to which the same relates :

(4.) The chairman of quarter sessions and the justices of the peace having jurisdiction in any county or riding assembled at such special sessions appointed in manner aforesaid, or at any adjournment of the same before the first day of December next after the passing of this Act, shall make an order dividing such county or riding of a county into polling districts, and appointing in each such polling district a place (in this section referred to as a "polling place") for taking the poll at contested elections of members to serve in Parliament for such county :

(5.) Every such division shall be made in such manner so that, as far as practicable, every building or place in such county in which petty sessions are at the time of the passing of this Act held shall be a polling place : provided always, that where it appears to the chairman and justices assembled at special sessions, that, for the purpose of affording full facilities for taking the poll at contested elections, there should be polling places in addition to such buildings or places where petty sessions are held as aforesaid, they shall appoint so many polling places in addition to such buildings or places as they may think necessary, and constitute a polling district for each such polling place :

(6.) Every such order shall specify the barony or

baronies, half barony or half baronies, town-
land or townlands, parish or parishes, and
places constituting each such polling district :

(7.) A copy of every such order shall forthwith
be sent by the clerk of the peace for such
county to the clerk of the said Privy Council,
who thereupon shall submit the same for
confirmation by the Lord Lieutenant and
Privy Council in Ireland, in the manner by
this Act provided, and such order shall not
be of any validity until the same has been so
confirmed :

(8.) Notice of the intended confirmation of any
such order shall be given by the clerk of the
said Privy Council at least one month before
the day fixed for such confirmation by the
publication of such notice and order in one
or more newspapers circulating within such
county or riding to which the order has
reference.

(9.) It shall be lawful for the Lord Lieutenant
and Privy Council, on the day fixed for the
intended confirmation of any such order, to
confirm the same as it stands, or with such
variation, alteration, or modification as may
seem fit : Provided always, that where any
person is dissatisfied with any such order it
shall be lawful for such person, within four-
teen days after the publication of the notice
of the intended confirmation of such order,
to appeal against the same, and such appeal
shall be in writing, stating the grounds
thereof, and shall be signed by such person,
and shall within such time be lodged with
the clerk of the Privy Council ; and it shall
be lawful for the Lord Lieutenant and Privy
Council, previous to the confirmation of any
such order, to hear and determine such appeal
against the same, and to make such order as
to the costs of such appeal as may seem
meet.

(10.) When any such order has been confirmed

as aforesaid, the clerk of the said Privy
Council shall transmit a copy of the same to
the clerk of the peace of the county to
which the same relates, and shall cause the
same to be published once in the Dublin
Gazette, and once in the newspaper in which
the notice of intended confirmation was
published :

(11.) The provisions of the Act of the session of
the twenty-seventh and twenty-eighth years
of the reign of Her present Majesty, chapter
twenty-two, for ascertaining the voters in
the new or altered polling districts referred
to in the ninth section of the said Act, and
for making separate lists of voters, and
otherwise in relation thereto, shall extend and
apply to every case in which any order in
relation to any county has been confirmed
under the authority of this section, in like
manner as if such sections were herein re-
enacted, and the polling districts to which
the same refer or apply had been polling
districts constituted under the authority of
this section : and the register of voters in
force in such county at the time of confirming such order as amended by the printed
books given into the custody of the sheriff
of such county in manner by the said Act
provided, and the said printed books, shall
be the register of persons entitled to vote at
any election of a member or members to
serve in Parliament which shall take place
in and for such county until the first day of
January next after the giving of the said
books as aforesaid : Provided always, that
in the construction of the said provisions,
the terms "the passing of this Act" and
the "said Act" shall respectively be construed to mean the confirming of any order
made under the authority of this section and
this Act :

(12.) At any election of a member or members

to serve in Parliament for any county to which any such order relates held after the confirming of any such order, and before the register of voters to be formed subsequently to the date of the confirming of such order under the provisions of this section shall be in force, the poll shall be taken as if no such order had been made :

(13.) All precepts, notices, and forms relating to the registration of voters shall be framed and expressed in such manner and form as may be necessary for the carrying the provisions of this Act into effect :

(14.) When the chairman of quarter sessions and justices of the peace having jurisdiction in any county or riding in Ireland, assembled at any general or quarter sessions in any division of such county or riding, are of opinion that for the purpose of affording further facilities for polling at contested elections there should be within such district polling places in addition to the places appointed in manner aforesaid, they may by resolution determine that at the next general or quarter sessions in such division of such county the necessity for such additional polling places shall be considered by the chairman and justices assembled at the same :

(15.) The clerk of the peace of such county shall, within five days after the making of such resolution, send a written or printed copy of the same to the chairman and to every justice of the peace having jurisdiction within the county to which the same relates, and shall cause a copy of such resolution to be published twice in each of two consecutive weeks in some newspaper circulated in such county :

(16.) The said chairman and justices assembled at such general or quarter sessions holden next after the making of such resolution shall consider whether additional polling places are necessary, and if they are of such opinion they may, by an order to be made in like manner and subject to the same provisions as to the making, confirming, and taking effect of the same as are in this section contained in relation to orders to be made at special sessions under the authority of the same, appoint such other places to be polling places as they shall think fit, and shall constitute polling districts for such polling places :

(17.) No election shall be questioned by reason of any polling district not having been constituted in conformity with the provisions of this Act, or by reason of any informality relative to any polling district :

(18.) When any day fixed for taking the poll at any election is the day fixed for the holding of the petty sessions court at any polling place, the court shall stand *ipso facto* adjourned till the next day, which shall in that case be the legal day for holding said court, and if that day be a Sunday or legal holiday, till the next day.

(19.) The term "the Lord Lieutenant" in this section shall mean the Lord Lieutenant of Ireland and the lords justices or other chief governors or governor of Ireland for the time being, and the term "chairman of quarter sessions" in this section shall include any person duly appointed to do the duty of such chairman during his sickness or absence.

The provisions of section 47 of the Corrupt Practices Act, 1883, relative to polling districts, do not apply to Ireland, except that "in the county of the town of Galway there shall be a polling station at Barna, and at such other places within the parliamentary borough of Galway as the town commissioners may appoint." 46 & 47 Vict. c. 51, s. 69.

19. Where the name of any person is required to be inserted in any list of voters for any ward of any city, town, or borough, under the provisions of section seven of the Act passed in the session of

Amendment of law as to voting in wards in certain boroughs.

Parliament held in the thirteenth and fourteenth years of the reign of Her present Majesty, chapter sixty-eight, as qualified in respect of any property qualification, or as the occupier of any lands, tenements, or hereditaments situate in whole or in part beyond the limits of such ward, then and in every such case the names so required to be inserted shall be placed in alphabetical order in a separate part of such list, to be styled "the list of rural or out-voters of such ward," and the property, lands, tenements, and hereditaments in respect of which such person is qualified as aforesaid shall for the purposes of the said Act and the Acts amending the same, in relation to the providing of booths and compartments within each ward of any city, town, or borough, and the voting therein of persons entitled to vote in respect of any such qualifications aforesaid, be deemed to constitute a separate ward : Provided always, that the name of any such person shall not be placed in such separate list if such person shall, in writing under his hand, object thereto, and if such objection is delivered to such clerk of the peace on or before the twenty-fifth day of August next preceding the making of such list under the provisions aforesaid, and in such case in relation to such person the provisions of this section shall not apply.

MUNICIPAL ELECTIONS IN SCOTLAND AND IRELAND.

Application to municipal election of enactments relating to the poll at parliamentary elections.

20. The poll at every contested municipal election shall, so far as circumstances admit, be conducted in the manner in which the poll is by this Act directed to be conducted at a contested parliamentary election, and, subject to the modifications expressed in the schedules annexed hereto, such provisions of this Act and of the said schedules as relate to or are concerned with a poll at a parliamentary election, shall apply to a poll at a contested municipal election : Provided as follows :

(1.) The term "returning officer" shall mean the mayor or other officer who, under the law relating to municipal elections, presides at such elections :

(2.) The term "petition questioning the election or return" shall mean any proceeding in which a municipal election can be questioned :

(3.) The mayor shall provide everything which in the case of a parliamentary election is required to be provided by the returning officer for the purpose of a poll :

(4.) All expenses shall be defrayed in manner provided by law with respect to the expenses of a municipal election :

(5.) No return shall be made to the Clerk of the Crown in Chancery :

(6.) Nothing in this Act shall be deemed to authorise the appointment of any agents of a candidate in a municipal election, but if in the case of a municipal election any agent of a candidate is appointed, and a notice in writing of such appointment is given to the returning officer, the provisions of this Act with respect to agents of candidates shall, so far as respects such agent, apply in the case of that election :

(7.) The provisions of this Act with respect to—
    (a.) The voting of a returning officer ; and
    (b.) The use of a room for taking a poll ; and
    (c.) The right to vote of persons whose names are on the register of voters :
shall not apply in the case of a municipal election.

A municipal election shall, except in so far as relates to the taking of the poll in the event of its being contested, be conducted in the manner in which it would have been conducted if this Act had not passed.

21. Assessors shall not be elected in any ward of any municipal borough, and a municipal election need not be held before the assessors or their deputies

Abolition of ward assessors.

but may be held before the mayor, aldermen or other returning officer only.

Alterations for application of Part II. of Ballot Act to Scotland.

22. This part of this Act shall apply to Scotland, subject to the following provisions :—

(1.) The term " mayor " shall mean the provost or other chief magistrate of a municipal borough, as defined by this Act.

(2.) All municipal elections shall be conducted in the same manner in all respects in which elections of councillors in the royal burghs contained in Schedule C to the Act of the session of the third and fourth years of the reign of King William the Fourth, chapter seventy-six, intituled " An Act to alter and amend the laws for the election of the Magistrates and Councillors of the Royal Burghs in Scotland," are directed to be conducted by the Acts in force at the time of the passing of this Act as amended by this Act ; and all such Acts shall apply to such elections accordingly.

Alteration for application of Part II. of Ballot Act to Ireland.

23. This part of this Act shall apply to Ireland, with the following modifications :—

(1.) The term " mayor " shall include the chairman of commissioners, chairman of municipal commissioners, chairman of town commissioners, and chairman of township commissioners :

25 Vict. c. 35.

(2.) The provisions of " The Municipal Corporation Act, 1859," following ; that is to say, section five and section six and section seven, except so much thereof as relates to the form of nomination papers, and section eight except so much thereof as relates to assessors, shall extend and apply to every municipal borough in Ireland, and shall be substituted for any provisions in force in relation to the nomination at municipal elections : Provided always that the term "councillor" in these sections shall for the purposes of this section include alderman, commissioner, municipal commissioner, town commissioner, township commissioner, or assessor of any municipal borough.

PERSONATION.

The following enactments shall be made with respect to personation at parliamentary and municipal elections :

A person shall for all purposes of the laws relating to parliamentary and municipal elections be deemed to be guilty of the offence of personation who at an election for a county or borough, or at a municipal election, applies for a ballot paper in the name of some other person, whether that name be that of a person living or dead or of a fictitious person, or who having voted once at any such election applies at the same election for a ballot paper in his own name.

It shall be the duty of the returning officer to institute a prosecution against any person whom he may believe to have been guilty of personation, or of aiding, abetting, counselling, or of procuring the commission of the offence of personation by any person, at the election for which he is returning officer, and the costs and expenses of the prosecutor and the witnesses in such case, together with compensation for their trouble and loss of time, shall be allowed by the court in the same manner in which courts are empowered to allow the same in case of felony.

The provisions of the Registration Act, specified in the Third Schedule to this Act, shall in England and Ireland respectively apply to personation under this Act in the same manner as they apply to a person who knowingly personates and falsely assumes to vote in the name of another person as mentioned in the said Acts.

Definition and punishment of personation contained in the Ballot Act.

Again by section 3 of the Corrupt Practices Act, 1883 (46 & 47 Vict. c. 51), and by section 1 of the Corrupt Practices Act, 1884, and section 75 of the Local Government Act, 1888, it is enacted that :—

A person who commits the offence of personation or the offence of aiding, abetting, counselling, and procuring the offence of personation shall be guilty of a corrupt practice, and by section 6 of the Corrupt Practices Act, 1883, (2) the offence of personation and aiding and abetting, &c., is declared to be felony and punishable upon indictment with two years' imprisonment with hard labour. The consequences of the provision of the law declaring personation of a corrupt practice are, that if it is shown that it has been committed by any agent of the sitting member, the latter will lose his seat on petition and be incapacitated for sitting for the same place for seven years. That is the consequence to the sitting member ; but so far as the person actually guilty of the crime is concerned he is liable to (1) two years' imprisonment with hard labour, (2) incapacity to sit in the House of Commons for any constituency for seven years, (3) incapacity of being registered and voting at any election (parliamentary or otherwise) for seven years, (4) incapacity for holding any public office for seven years, and (5) if a barrister, solicitor, justice of the peace, or licensed victualler further measures of severity may be taken against him.

As to application for exemption from corrupt practices *see ex parte*, Perry 48 J. P. 824; as to the time within which particulars of corrupt practices must be delivered in *see* Lenham *v.* Barber, 10 Q.B.D. 293; as to applications for relief from the consequences of *illegal* practices *see ex parte* Wilkes 16 Q.B.D. 114, 55 L.J.Q.B. 576; as to convictions for corrupt practices *see* R. *v.* Stroulger 17 Q.B.D. 327.

Vote to be struck off for bribery, treating, or undue influence. (Ballot Act) 25. (*a*) Where a candidate, on the trial of an election petition claiming the seat for any person, is proved to have been guilty, by himself or by any person on his behalf, of bribery, (*b*) treating or undue influence in respect of any person who voted at such election, or where any person retained or employed (*c*) for reward by or on behalf of such candidate for all or any of the purposes of such election, as agent

(*a*.) This section refers exclusively to the procedure on a scrutiny with a view to the unseating of the respondent and the seating of the petitioner. The first object will be attained by proving a *single* case of bribery, treating, unduo influence, personation, or, under the Corrupt Practices Acts of 1883 and 1884, any ill g d practice, to have b en committed by the respondent. or any one of his agents; but the petitioner is not entitled to be declared elected until by striking bad votes off his opponent's poll · r adding votes, improperly disallowed by the returning officer, to his own he obtains a clear majority of legal votes. The above section provides for votes being struck off the respondent's poll in the cases which fall within it.

(b.) In MALCOLM *r.* PARRY (L. R. 9, C. P. 610) it was proved that a large number of voters received a quantity of coal from the respondent's agents just before the election. The Court of Common Pleas held that the above facts constituted a *primâ facie* case of corruption against the voters, upon which, in the absence of evidence in rebuttal, the votes must be struck off. Under this section a vote is struck off the respondent's poll upon proof that the voter was bribed or treated by the respondent's agent *without any inquiry as to how in fact he voted* (Per Lord Coleridge, C.J., in MALCOLM *c.* PARRY *supra*).

(c.) In the DOWN CASE (3 O'M. & H. 115) it was held that the drivers of fly and cabs used in connection with the election did not come within the section; but now it is unlawful to pay for any carriages or traps used in the conveyance of electors to or from the poll (46 & 47 Vict. c. 51, s. 7, and 47 & 48 Vict. c 70, s. 10).

clerk, messenger, or in any other employment, is proved on such trial to have voted at such election, there shall, on a scrutiny, be struck off from the number of votes appearing to have been given to such candidate one vote for every person who voted at such election and is proved to have been so bribed, treated, or unduly influenced, or so retained or employed for reward as aforesaid.

26. This part of this Act shall apply to Scotland subject to the following provision :—

The offence of personation shall be deemed to be a crime and offence, and the rules of the law of Scotland with respect to apprehension, detention, precognition, commitment, and bail shall apply thereto, and any person accused thereof may be brought to trial in the court of justiciary, whether in Edinburgh or on circuit, at the instance of the Lord Advocate,

Alterations in Act as applying to Scotland.

3

or before the sheriff court, at the instance of the procurator fiscal.

Construction of part of Ballot Act. 27. This part of this Act, so far as regards parliamentary elections, shall be construed as one with "The Parliamentary Elections Act, 1868," and shall apply to an election for a university or combination of universities.

FIRST SCHEDULE TO THE BALLOT ACT, 1872.

PART I.—Rules for Parliamentary Elections.

Election.

1. The returning officer shall, in the case of a county election, within two days after the day on which he receives the writ, and in the case of a borough election on the day on which he receives the writ or the following day, give public notice, between the hours of nine in the morning and four in the afternoon, of the day on which and the place at which he will proceed to an election, and of the time appointed for the election, and of the day on which the poll will be taken in case the election is contested, and of the time and place at which forms of nomination papers may be obtained, and in the case of a county election shall send one of such notices by post under cover, to the postmaster of the principal post office of each polling place in the county, endorsed with the words " Notice of election," and the same shall be forwarded free of charge ; and the postmaster receiving the same shall forthwith publish the same in the manner in which post office notices are usually published.

2. The day of election shall be fixed by the returning officer as follows ; that is to say, in the case of an election for a county or a district borough not later than the ninth day after the day on which he receives the writ, with an interval of not less than three clear days between the day on which he gives the notice and the day of election ; and in the case of an election for any borough other than a district borough not later than the fourth day after the day

on which he receives the writ, with an interval of not less than two clear days between the day on which he gives the notice and the day of election.

In the LONGFORD CASE (2 O'M. & H. 7) an irregularity was suggested in regard to the day on which the election was held, and it was submitted the election was void on that ground. Fitzgerald, J. expressed an opinion adverse to this contention, but it became unnecessary to decide the point.

3. The place of election shall be a convenient room situate in the town in which such election would have been held if this Act had not passed, or where the election would not have been held in a town, then situate in such town in the county as the returning officer may from time to time determine as being in his opinion most convenient for the electors.

4. The time appointed for the election shall be such two hours between the hours of ten in the forenoon and three in the afternoon as may be appointed by the returning officer, and the returning officer shall attend during those two hours and for one hour after.

5. Each candidate shall be nominated by a separate nomination paper, but the same electors or any of them may subscribe as many nomination papers as there are vacancies to be filled, but no more.

6. Each candidate shall be described in the nomination paper in such manner as in the opinion of the returning officer is calculated to sufficiently identify such candidate ; the description shall include his name, his abode, and his rank, profession, or calling, and his surname shall come first in the list of his names. No objection to a nomination paper on the ground of the description of the candidate therein being insufficient, or not being in compliance with this rule. shall be allowed or deemed valid, unless such objection is made by the returning officer, or by some other person, at or immediately after the time of the delivery of the nomination paper.

7. The returning officer shall supply a form of nomination paper to any registered elector requiring the same during such two hours as the returning officer may fix, between the hours of ten in the morning and two in the afternoon on each day intervening between the day on which notice

of the election was given and the day of election, and during the time appointed for the election ; but nothing in this Act shall render obligatory the use of a nomination paper supplied by the returning officer, so, however, that the paper be in the form prescribed by this Act.

8. The nomination papers shall be delivered to the returning officer at the place of election during the time appointed for the election ; and the candidate nominated by each nomination paper, and his proposer and seconder, and one other person selected by the candidate, and no person other than aforesaid, shall, except for the purpose of assisting the returning officer, be entitled to attend the proceedings during the time appointed for the election.

9. If the election is contested the returning officer shall, as soon as practicable after adjourning the election, give public notice of the day on which the poll will be taken, and of the candidates described as in their respective nomination papers, and of the names of the persons who subscribe the nomination paper of each candidate, and of the order in which the names of the candidates will be printed in the ballot paper, and, in the case of an election for a county, deliver to the postmaster of the principal post office of the town in which is situate the place of election a paper, signed by himself, containing the names of the candidates nominated, and stating the day on which the poll is to be taken, and the postmaster shall forward the information contained in such paper by telegraph, free of charge, to the several postal telegraph offices situate in the county for which the election is to be held, and such information shall be published forthwith at each such office in the manner in which post-office notices are usually published.

10. If any candidate nominated during the time appointed for the election is withdrawn in pursuance of this Act, the returning officer shall give public notice of the name of such candidate, and the names of the persons who subscribed the nomination paper of such candidate, as well as of the candidates who stood nominated or were elected.

11. The returning officer shall, on the nomination paper being delivered to him, forthwith publish notice of the name of the person nominated as a candidate, and of the names of his proposer and seconder, by placarding or causing to

be placarded the names of the candidate and his proposer and seconder in a conspicuous position outside the building in which the room is situate appointed for the election.

12. A person shall not be entitled to have his name inserted in any ballot paper as a candidate unless he has been nominated in manner provided by this Act, and every person whose nomination paper has been delivered to the returning officer during the time appointed for the election shall be deemed to have been nominated in manner provided by this Act, unless objection be made to his nomination paper by the returning officer or some other person before the expiration of the time appointed for the election or within one hour afterwards.

13. The returning officer shall decide on the validity of every objection made to a nomination paper, and his decision, if disallowing the objection, shall be final ; but if allowing the same, shall be subject to reversal on petition questioning the election or return.

The Poll.

14. The poll shall take place on such day as the returning officer may appoint, not being in the case of an election for a county or a district borough less than two nor more than six clear days, and not being in the case of an election for a borough other than a district borough more than three clear days after the day fixed for the election.

By the Elections (Hours of Poll) Act, 1885 (48 Vict. cap. 10), it is enacted that at all county and borough elections, whether in the metropolis or the provinces, the poll is to be open from 8 a.m. to 8 p.m. The effect upon the election of failing to open the poll at the proper time is discussed later on at pp. 64-65; but with regard to the effect of failing to close the poll punctually at the time appointed, the best opinion seems to be that no voting paper should be given out to a voter after the clock has struck, b t if a voter has received a paper before, he ought to be allowed to mark and deposit it in the ballot box after the time. (*See* "Arnold on Municipal Corporations," 3rd ed. p. 306). In an Irish case of GRIBBIN *v.* KIRKER (7 Ir., C. L. 30), the election was upset on account of the action of the returning officer in receiving votes after 4 p.m.; but the irregularity was apparently of a gross character, because the report states votes were given up to 5 o'clock.

15. At every polling place the returning officer shall provide a sufficient number of polling stations for the accommodation of the electors entitled to vote at such polling place, and shall distribute the polling stations amongst those electors in such manner as he thinks most convenient, provided that in a district borough there shall be at least one polling station at each contributory place of such borough.

16. Each polling station shall be furnished with such number of compartments, in which the voters can mark their votes screened from observation, as the returning officer thinks necessary, so that at least one compartment be provided for every one hundred and fifty electors entitled to vote at such polling station.

17. A separate room or separate booth may contain a separate polling station, or several polling stations may be constructed in the same room or booth.

18. No person shall be admitted to vote at any polling station except the one allotted to him.

19. The returning officer shall give public notice of the situation of polling stations and the description of voters entitled to vote at each station, and of the mode in which electors are to vote.

20. The returning officer shall provide each polling station with materials for voters to mark the ballot papers, with instruments for stamping thereon the official mark, and with copies of the register of voters, or such part thereof as contain the names of the voters allotted to vote at such station. He shall keep the official mark secret, and an interval of not less than seven years shall intervene between the use of the same official mark at elections for the same county or borough.

21. The returning officer shall appoint a presiding officer to preside at each station, and the officer so appointed shall keep order at his station, shall regulate the number of electors to be admitted at a time, and shall exclude all other persons except the clerks, the agents of the candidates and the constables on duty.

In addition the candidate is entitled to be in the polling station. In CLEMENTSON v. MASON, L. R. 10, C. P. 209, it was decided that a candidate at a parliamentary or municipal election has a general right to be present in a polling station at the election, and not merely a qualified right to be present for the purpose of undertaking the duties of an agent, or of assisting his agent.

22. Every ballot paper shall contain a list of the candidates described as in their respective nomination papers, and arranged alphabetically in the order of their surnames, and (if there are two or more candidates with the same surname) of their other names : it shall be in the form set forth in the Second Schedule to this Act or as near thereto as circumstances admit, and shall be capable of being folded up.

The name of the *same* candidate twice nominated ought only to appear once on the nomination paper. NORTHCOTE *v.* PULSFORD, L. R. 10, C. P. 483.

23. Every ballot box shall be so constructed that the ballot papers can be introduced therein, but cannot be withdrawn therefrom, without the box being unlocked. The presiding officer at any polling station, just before the commencement of the poll, shall show the ballot box empty to such persons, if any, as may be present in such station, so that they may see that it is empty, and shall then lock it up, and place his seal upon it in such manner as to prevent its being opened without breaking such seal, and shall place it in his view for the receipt of ballot papers, and keep it so locked and sealed.

24. Immediately before a ballot paper is delivered to an elector, it shall be marked on both sides with the official mark, either stamped or perforated, and the number, name, and description of the elector as stated in the copy of the register shall be called out, and the number of such elector shall be marked on the counterfoil, and a mark shall be placed in the register against the number of the elector, to denote that he has received a ballot paper, but without showing the particular ballot paper which he has received.

See PICKERING *v.* JAMES, quoted at p. 18, as to the extent of a presiding officer's duty and liability under this rule.

25. The elector, on receiving the ballot paper, shall forthwith proceed into one of the compartments in the polling station, and there mark his paper, and fold it up so as to conceal his vote, and shall then put his ballot paper, so

folded up, into the ballot box ; he shall vote without undue delay, and shall quit the polling station as soon as he has put his ballot paper into the ballot box.

26. The presiding officer, on the application of any voter who is incapacitated by blindness or other physical cause from voting in manner prescribed by this Act, or (if the poll be taken on Saturday) of any voter who declares that he is of the Jewish persuasion, and objects on religious grounds to vote in manner prescribed by this Act, or of any voter who makes such a declaration as hereinafter mentioned that he is unable to read, shall, in the presence of the agents of the candidates, cause the vote of such voter to be marked on a ballot paper in manner directed by such voter, and the ballot paper to be placed in the ballot box, and the name and number on the register of voters of every voter whose vote is marked in pursuance of this rule, and the reason why it is so marked, shall be entered on a list, in this Act called " the list of votes marked by the presiding officer."

The said declaration, in this Act referred to as " the declaration of inability to read," shall be made by the voter at the time of polling, before the presiding officer, who shall attest it in the form hereinafter mentioned, and no fee, stamp, or other payment sha'l be charged in respect of such declaration, and the said declaration shall be given to the presiding officer at the time of voting.

27. If a person representing himself to be a particular elector named on the register, applies for a ballot paper after another person has voted as such elector, the applicant shall, upon duly answering the questions and taking the oath permitted by law to be asked of and to be administered to voters at the time of polling, be entitled to mark a ballot paper in the same manner as any other voter, but the ballot paper (in this Act called a tendered ballot paper) shall be of a colour differing from the other ballot papers, and, instead of being put into the ballot box, shall be given to the presiding officer and endorsed by him with the name of the voter and his number in the register of voters, and set aside in a separate packet, and shall not be counted by the returning officer. And the name of the voter and his number on the register shall be entered on a list, in this Act called the tendered votes list.

Upon a scrutiny, the tendered vote would be counted as soon as right of the person who tendered it to vote was established.

28. A voter who has inadvertently dealt with his ballot paper in such manner that it cannot be conveniently used as a ballot paper, may, on delivering to the presiding officer the ballot paper so inadvertently dealt with, and proving the fact of the inadvertence to the satisfaction of the presiding officer, obtain another ballot paper in the place of the ballot paper so delivered up (in this Act called a spoilt ballot paper), and the spoilt ballot paper shall be immediately cancelled.

29. The presiding officer of each station, as soon as practicable after the close of the poll, shall, in the presence of the agents of the candidates, make up into separate packets sealed with his own seal and the seals of such agents of the candidates as desire to affix their seals,—

(1.) Each ballot box in use at his station, unopened but with the key attached ; and

(2.) The unused and spoilt ballot papers, placed together ; and

(3.) The tendered ballot papers ; and

(4.) The marked copies of the register of voters and the counterfoils of the ballot papers ; and

(5.) The tendered votes list, and the list of votes marked by the presiding officer, and a statement of the number of the voters whose votes are so marked by the presiding officer under the heads " physical incapacity," " Jews." and " unable to read," and the declarations of inability to read :

and shall deliver such packets to the returning officer.

30. The packets shall be accompanied by a statement made by such presiding officer, showing the number of ballot papers entrusted to him, and accounting for them under the heads of ballot papers in the ballot box, unused, spoilt, and tendered ballot papers, which statement is in this Act referred to as the ballot paper account.

Counting Votes.

31. The candidates may respectively appoint agents to attend the counting of the votes.

32. The returning officer shall make arrangements for counting the votes in the presence of the agents of the candidates as soon as practicable after the close of the poll, and shall give to the agents of the candidates appointed to attend at the counting of the votes notice in writing of the time and place at which he will begin to count the same.

33. The returning officer, his assistants and clerks, and the agents of the candidates, and no other person, except with the sanction of the returning officer, may be present at the counting of the votes.

The candidates are entitled to be present. Rule 51, and CLEMENTSON *v.* MASON, quoted at p. 39.

34. Before the returning officer proceeds to count the votes, he shall, in the presence of the agents of the candidates, open each ballot box, and, taking out the papers therein, shall count and record the number thereof, and then mix together the whole of the ballot papers contained in the ballot boxes. The returning officer, while counting and recording the number of ballot papers, and counting the votes, shall keep the ballot papers with their faces upwards, and taking all proper precautions for preventing any person from seeing the numbers printed on the backs of such papers.

35. The returning officer shall, so far as practicable, proceed continuously with counting the votes, allowing only time for refreshment, and excluding (except so far as he and the agents otherwise agree) the hours between seven o'clock at night and nine o'clock on the succeeding morning. During the excluded time the returning officer shall place the ballot papers and other documents relating to the election under his own seal and the seals of such of the agents of the candidates as desire to affix their seals, and shall otherwise take proper precautions for the security of such papers and documents.

36. The returning officer shall indorse "rejected" on any ballot paper which he may reject as invalid, and shall add to the indorsement "rejection objected to" if an objection be in fact made by any agent to his decision. The returning officer shall report to the Clerk of the Crown in

Chancery the number of ballot papers rejected, and not counted by him under the several heads of—

1. Want of official mark ;
2. Voting for more candidates than entitled to ;
3. Writing or mark by which voter could be identified ;
4. Unmarked or void for uncertainty ;

and shall, on request, allow any agents of the candidates, before such report is sent, to copy it.

The law is now settled that a ballot paper is to be rejected by the returning officer, and if admitted by him, is to be struck off upon a scrutiny, " if there be substantially a want of any mark, or a mark which leaves it uncertain whether the voter intended to vote at all, or for which candidate he intended to vote, or if there be marks indicating that the voter has voted for too many candidates, or a writing or a mark by which the voter can be identified ; or to put the matter affirmatively, the paper must be marked so as to show that the voter intended to vote for some one, and so as to show for which of the candidates he intended to vote. It must not be marked so as to show that he intended to vote for more candidates than he is entitled, nor so as to leave it uncertain whether he intended to vote at all, or for which candidate he intended to vote, nor so as to make it possible, by seeing the paper itself, or by reference to other available facts, to identify the voter." WOODWARD *v.* SARSONS, L. R. 10, C. P. 748. Accordingly the following papers have been held void :—(1) A paper on which the presiding officer marked the number of the voter in the register, (for thereby the voter might be identified) (WOODWARD *v.* SARSONS *supra*) ; (2) a paper with the name of the voter written thereon (*ibid.*) ; (3) a paper with the name of the candidate voted for written opposite to the name of the latter (*ibid.*) ; (4) a paper with the addition of a mark like ' m " to the cross (*ibid.*) ; (5) a paper having two strokes on the back in addition to the ordinary cross (WIGTOWN, 2 O'M. & H., p. 219) ; (6) a paper marked on the back with a cross exactly against the name of a candidate visible through the paper, but not marked with any cross on the face (BERWICK, 3 O'M. & H., 182).

On the other hand, in the absence of any evidence of connivance, prearrangement, or of the irregularity being intended to afford a means of identifying the voter, the following papers have been held good :—(1) A paper marked with two or more crosses (WOODWARD *v.* SARSONS *supra*) ; (2) a paper marked with a single stroke only opposite a candidate's name (*ibid.*) ; (3) or with a straight line or a mark like an imperfect letter P in addition to the cross (*ibid.*) ; (4) or with a star in lieu of a cross (*ibid.*) or with a cross blurred or marked with a tremulous hand (*ibid.*) ; (5) or with a cross placed on the left-hand side of the ballot paper (*ibid.*) ; (6) or with a pencil line drawn longitudinally through the name of the candidate not voted for (*ibid.*) ; (7) a paper torn longitudinally through the centre (*ibid.*) ; (8) a paper marked with a cross on the right-hand side of the paper and outside the proper column (ATH-LONE, 2 O'M. & H., 186) ; (9) a paper marked with a cross made, not with a pencil. but with ink, a burnt stick, or a finger nail (BER-WICK, 3 O'M. & H , 178, and WIGTOWN, 2 O'M. & H., 223) ; and (10) a paper marked with a cross extending largely into the space opposite the name of one candidate, but having the point of intersection within the space opposite the name of the other candidate to whom the vote was awarded (BERWICK *supra*).

Lopes and Hawkins, J.J., differed on the question—Whether a paper marked with a cross on the top left-hand corner, not opposite but nearer to the name of the first candidate on the paper, was a good vote for that candidate (BERWICK *supra*).

37. Upon the completion of the counting, the returning officer shall seal up in separate packets the counted and rejected ballot papers. He shall not open the sealed packet of tendered ballot papers or marked copy of the register of voters and counterfoils, but shall proceed, in the presence of the agents of the candidates, to verify the ballot paper account given by each presiding officer by comparing it with the number of ballot papers recorded by him as aforesaid, and the unused and spoiled ballot papers in his possession and the tendered votes list, and shall re-seal each sealed packet after examination. The returning officer shall report to the Clerk of the Crown in Chancery the result of such verification, and shall, on request, allow any agents of the candidates, before such report is sent, to copy it.

38. Lastly, the returning officer shall forward to the Clerk of the Crown in Chancery (in manner in which the poll books are by any existing enactment required to be forwarded to such clerk, or as near thereto as circumstances admit) all the packets of ballot papers in his possession, together with the said reports, the ballot paper accounts, tendered votes lists, lists of votes marked by the presiding officer, statements relating thereto, declarations of inability to read, and packets of counterfoils, and marked copies of registers, sent by each presiding officer, endorsing on each packet a description of its contents and the date of the election to which they relate, and the name of the county or borough for which such election was held ; and the term poll book in any such enactment shall be construed to include any document forwarded in pursuance of this rule.

39. The Clerk of the Crown shall retain for a year all documents relating to an election forwarded to him in pursuance of this Act, by a returning officer, and then, unless otherwise directed by an order of the House of Commons, or of one of Her Majesty's Superior Courts, shall cause them to be destroyed.

40. No person shall be allowed to inspect any rejected ballot papers in the custody of the Clerk of the Crown in Chancery, except under the order of the House of Commons, or under the order of one of Her Majesty's Superior Courts, to be granted by such court on being satisfied by evidence on oath that the inspection or production of such ballot papers is required for the purpose of instituting or maintaining a prosecution for an offence in relation to ballot papers, or for the purpose of a petition questioning an election or return ; and any such order for the inspection or production of ballot papers may be made subject to such conditions as to persons, time, place, and mode of inspection or production as the House or court making the same may think expedient, and shall be obeyed by the Clerk of the Crown in Chancery. Any power given to a court by this rule may be exercised by any judge of such court at Chambers.

41. No person shall, except by order of the House of Commons or any tribunal having cognizance of petitions complaining of undue returns or undue elections, open the sealed packet of counterfoils after the same has been once sealed up, or be allowed to inspect any counted ballot papers in the custody of the Clerk of the Crown in Chancery ; such order may be made subject to such conditions as to persons, time, place, and mode of opening or inspection as the House or tribunal making the order may think expedient ; provided that on making and carrying into effect any such order, care shall be taken that the mode in which any particular elector has voted shall not be discovered until he has been proved to have voted, and his vote has been declared by a competent court to be invalid.

42. All documents forwarded by a returning officer in pursuance of this Act to the Clerk of the Crown in Chancery, other than ballot papers and counterfoils, shall be open to public inspection at such time and under such

regulations as may be prescribed by the Clerk of the Crown in Chancery, with the consent of the Speaker of the House of Commons, and the Clerk of the Crown shall supply copies of or extracts from the said documents to any person demanding the same, on payment of such fees, and subject to such regulations as may be sanctioned by the Treasury.

Leave to inspect the marked register of voters will be granted whether the petition against the return of a candidate at a parliamentary election does or does not pray for a scrutiny, JAMES *v.* HENDERSON, 43 L. J., C. P. 238; 30 L.T. 527. See also STOWE *v.* JOLLIFFE (No. 1), 43 L. J., C. P. 173.

43. Where an order is made for the production by the Clerk of the Crown in Chancery of any document in his possession relating to any specified election, the production by such clerk or his agent of the document ordered, in such manner as may be directed by such order, or by a rule of the court having power to make such order, shall be conclusive evidence that such document relates to the specified election ; and any endorsement appearing on any packet of ballot papers produced by such Clerk of the Crown or his agent shall be evidence of such papers being what they are stated to be by the endorsement   The production from proper custody of a ballot paper purporting to have been used at any election, and of a counterfoil marked with the same printed number and having a number marked thereon in writing, shall be *primâ facie* evidence that the person who voted by such ballot paper was the person who at the time of such election had affixed to his name in the register of voters at such election the same number as the number written on such counterfoil.

General Provisions.

44. The return of a member or members elected to serve in Parliament for any county or borough shall be made by a certificate of the names of such member or members under the hand of the returning officer endorsed on the writ of election for such county or borough, and such certificate shall have effect and be dealt with in like manner as the return under the existing law, and the returning officer may,

if he think fit, deliver the writ with such certificate endorsed to the postmaster of the principal post office of the place of election, or his deputy, and in that case he shall take a receipt from the postmaster or his deputy for the same ; and such postmaster or his deputy shall then forward the same by the first post, free of charge, under cover, to the Clerk of the Crown, with the words " Election Writ and Return " endorsed thereon.

45. The returning office shall, as soon as possible, give public notice of the names of the candidates elected, and, in the case of a contested election, of the total number of votes given for each candidate, whether elected or not.

46. Where the returning officer is required or authorised by this Act to give any public notice, he shall carry such requirement into effect by advertisements, placards, hand-bills, or such other means as he thinks best calculated to afford information to the electors.

47. The returning officer may, if he think fit, preside at any polling station, and the provisions of this Act relating to a presiding officer shall apply to such returning officer with the necessary modifications as to things to be done by the returning officer to the presiding officer, or the presiding officer to the returning officer.

48. In the case of a contested election for any county or borough, the returning officer may, in addition to any clerks, appoint competent persons to assist him in counting the votes.

49. No person shall be appointed by a returning officer for the purposes of an election who has been employed by any other person in or about the election.

50. The presiding officer may do, by the clerks appointed to assist him, any act which he is required or authorised to do by this Act at a polling station except ordering the arrest, exclusion, or ejection from the polling station of any person.

51. A candidate may himself undertake the duties which any agent of his if appointed might have undertaken, or may assist his agent in the performance of such duties, and may be present at any place at which his agent may, in pursuance of this Act, attend.

52. The name and address of every agent of a candidate appointed to attend the counting of the votes shall be trans-

mitted to the returning officer one clear day at the least
before the opening of the poll ; and the returning officer
may refuse to admit to the place where the votes are counted
any agent whose name and address has not been so transmitted, notwithstanding that his appointment may be otherwise valid, and any notice required to be given to an agent
by the returning officer may be delivered at or sent by post
to such address.

53. If any person appointed an agent by a candidate for
the purposes of attending at the polling station or at the
counting of the votes dies, or becomes incapable of acting
during the time of the election, the candidate may appoint
another agent in his place, and shall forthwith give to the
returning officer notice in writing of the name and address
of the agent so appointed.

54. Every returning officer, and every officer, clerk, or
agent authorised to attend at a polling station, or at the
counting of the votes, shall, before the opening of the poll,
make a statutory declaration of secrecy, in the presence, if
he is the returning officer, of a justice of the peace, and if he
is any other officer or an agent, of a justice of the peace or
of the returning officer ; but no such returning officer,
officer, clerk, or agent as aforesaid shall, save as aforesaid,
be required as such, to make any declaration or take any
oath on the occasion of any election.

55. Where in this Act any expressions are used requiring
or authorising or inferring that any act or thing is to be
done in the presence of the agents of the candidates, such
expressions shall be deemed to refer to the presence of such
agents of the candidates as may be authorised to attend,
and as have in fact attended, at the time and place where such
act or thing is being done, and the non-attendance of any
agents or agent at such time and place shall not, if such
act or thing be otherwise duly done, in anywise invalidate
the act or thing done.

56. In reckoning time for the purposes of this Act,
Sunday, Christmas Day, Good Friday, and any day set
apart for a public fast or public thanksgiving, shall be excluded ; and where anything is required by this Act to be
done on any day which falls on the above-mentioned days
such things may be done on the next day, unless it is one
of the days excluded as above-mentioned.

57. In this Act—

The expression "district borough" means the borough of Monmouth and any of the boroughs specified in Schedule E to the Act of the session of the second and third years of the reign of King William the Fourth, chapter forty-five, intituled "An Act to amend the Representation of the People in England and Wales ; " and

The expression "polling place" means, in the case of a borough, such borough or any part thereof in which a separate booth is required or authorised by law to be provided ; and

The expression "agents of the candidates," used in relation to a polling station, means agents appointed in pursuance of section eighty-five of the Act of the session of the sixth and seventh years of the reign of Her present Majesty, chapter eighteen.

Modifications in Application of Part I. of Schedule to Scotland.

58. In Scotland, the place of election shall be a convenient room situate in the town in which the writ for the election would, if this Act had not passed, have been proclaimed.

59. In Scotland, the candidates may respectively appoint agents to attend at the polling stations. The ballot papers and other documents other than the return required to be sent to and kept by the Clerk of the Crown in Chancery, shall, in Scotland, be kept by the sheriff clerks of the respective counties in which the returns (including those for burghs) are made, and the provisions of this schedule relating thereto shall be construed as if the sheriff clerk were substituted for Clerk of the Crown in Chancery.

60. In Scotland, the term "district borough" shall mean the combined burghs and towns specified in Schedule E of the Act of the session of the second and third years of the reign of King William the Fourth, chapter sixty-five, intituled "An Act to amend the Representation of the People in Scotland ;" and in Schedule A of the Representation of the People (Scotland) Act, 1868.

61. The provisions of the Act of the session of the second and third years of the reign of King William the Fourth, chapter sixty-five, intituled "An Act to amend the Representation of the People in Scotland," in so far as they relate to the fixing and announcement of the day of election, the interval to elapse between the receipt of the writ and the day of election, the period of adjournment for taking the poll in the case of Orkney and Shetland, and of the district of burghs comprising Kirkwall, Wick, Dornoch, Dingwall, Tain, and Cromarty, and to the keeping open of the poll for two consecutive days in the case of Orkney and Shetland shall remain in full force and effect, anything in this Act or any other Act of Parliament now in force notwithstanding ; but nothing herein contained shall be construed to exclude Orkney and Shetland or Orkney or Shetland, or the said district of burghs, or any of the burghs in the said district, from any of the benefits and obligations of the other portions of this Act.

Modifications in Application of Part I. of Schedule to Ireland.

62. The expression "Clerk of the Crown in Chancery" in this schedule shall mean, as regards Ireland, "the Clerk of the Crown and Hanaper in Ireland."

63. A presiding officer at a polling station in a county in Ireland need not be a freeholder of the county.

PART II.

RULES FOR MUNICIPAL ELECTIONS IN SCOTLAND AND IRELAND.

64. In the application of the provisions of this schedule to municipal elections the following modifications shall be made :—

(*a*.) The expression "register of voters" means the burgess roll of the burgesses of the borough, or, in the case of an election for the ward of a borough, the ward list; and the mayor shall provide true copies of such register for each polling station :

(*b*.) All ballot papers and other documents which, in the case of a parliamentary election, are forwarded to the Clerk of the Crown in Chancery shall be delivered to the town clerk of the municipal borough in which the election is held, and shall be kept by him among the records of the borough ; and the provisions of part one of this schedule with respect to the inspection, production, and destruction of such ballot papers and documents, and to the copies of such documents, shall apply respectively to the ballot papers and documents so in the custody of the town clerk, with these modifications ; namely,

(*a*.) An order of the county court having jurisdiction in the borough, or any part thereof, or of any tribunal in which a municipal election is questioned, shall be substituted for an order of the House of Commons, or of one of Her Majesty's Superior Courts ; but an appeal from such county court may be had in like manner as in other cases in such county court ;

(*b*.) The regulations for the inspection of documents and the fees for the supply of copies

of documents of which copies are directed to be
supplied, shall be prescribed by the council of the
borough with the consent of one of her Majesty's
Principal Secretaries of State ; and, subject as
aforesaid, the town clerk, in respect of the custody
and destruction of the ballot papers and other
documents coming into his possession, in pursuance of this Act, shall be subject to the
directions of the council of the borough ;

(c.) Nothing in this schedule with respect to
the day of the poll shall apply to a municipal
election.

In REG. *v.* BEARDSALL, 1 Q. B. D. 452, it was decided that a county
court judge could make an order for the production of the rejected
ballot papers used at a municipal election, in aid of a prosecution for
an offence against the Ballot Act.

65. In part two of this schedule as applying to
Scotland—

The expression " register of voters," means the register,
list, or roll of persons entitled to vote in a municipal
election made up according to the law for the time
being in force.

The expression " county court " means the sheriff
court.

The expression " town clerk " includes the clerk
appointed by the Commissioners of Police under the
Act of the session of the thirteenth and fourteenth
years of the reign of Her present Majesty, chapter
thirty-three, intituled " An Act to make more
effectual provision for regulating the police of towns
and populous places in Scotland, and for paving,
draining, cleansing, lighting, and improving the
same," and of the General Police and Improvement
(Scotland) Act, 1862.

66. In part two of this schedule as applying to
Ireland—

The expression " register of voters," in addition to the
meaning specified in such part, means, in relation

to any municipal borough subject to the provisions of a Local Act requiring an annual revision of the lists of voters at municipal elections, the register of voters made in conformity with the said provisions of such Local Act, and in relation to municipal boroughs to which Part II. of the Local Government (Ireland) Act, 1871, applies, the list to be made under the provisions of section twenty-seven of the said Act, and in relation to other municipal boroughs a list which the town clerk of every municipal borough is hereby authorised and directed to make, in like manner in every respect as if the provisions of the said section were applicable to and in force within such municipal borough.

The expression "county court" means the Civil Bill Court.

The expression "town clerk" includes clerk to the commissioners, municipal commissioners, town commissioners, or township commissioners of any municipal borough, and any person executing the duties of such town clerk.

The expression "council of the borough" includes commissioners, municipal commissioners, and town commissioners of the town, and township commissioners of the township.

The expression "one of Her Majesty's Principal Secretaries of State" means the Chief Secretary of the Lord Lieutenant of Ireland.

SECOND SCHEDULE.

Note.—The forms contained in this schedule, or forms as nearly resembling the same as circumstances will admit, shall be used in all cases to which they refer and are applicable, and when so used shall be sufficient in law.

Writ for a County or Borough at a Parliamentary Election.

°Victoria, by the Grace of God, of the United Kingdom of Great Britain and Ireland, Queen, Defender of the Faith, to the † of the county [*or* borough] of greeting :

‡ Whereas by the advice of our Council we have ordered a Parliament to be holden at Westminster on the day of next. We command you that, notice of the time and place of election being first duly given, you do cause election to be made according to law of members [*or* a member] to serve in Parliament for the said county [*or* the division of the said county, *or* the borough, *or as the case may be*] of § and that you do cause the names of such members [*or* member] when so elected, whether they [*or* he] be present or absent, to be certified to us, in our Chancery, without delay.

Witness ourself at Westminster, the day of in the year of our reign, and in the year of our Lord 18 .

Label or Direction of Writ.

To the † of

A writ of a new election of members [*or* member] for the said county [*or* division of a county *or* borough, *or as the case may be*].

Endorsement.

Received the within writ on the day of 18
(Signed) **A.B.,**
High Sheriff [*or* Sheriff, *or* Mayor, *or as the case may be*].

*The name of the Sovereign may be altered when necessary.

†Insert "sheriff" or other returning officer.

‡This preamble to be omitted except in case of a general election.

§Except in a general election insert herein the place of A.B., deceased, or otherwise, stating the cause of vacancy.

Certificate endorsed on the Writ.

I hereby certify, that the members [or member] elected
for   in pursuance of the within-written
writ, are [or is] *A.B.* of   in the county
of   and *C.D.* of   in
the county of

(Signed)   A.B.,

High Sheriff [or Sheriff, *or* Mayor, *or as the case may be*].
Note.—A separate writ will be issued for each county as
defined for the purposes of a parliamentary election.

Form of Notice of Parliamentary Election.

The returning officer of the   of
will, on the   day of   now next ensuing,
between the hours of   and   , proceed to
the nomination, and, if there is no opposition, to the
election, of a member [or members] for the said county
[or division of a county *or* borough] at the °

Forms of nomination paper may be obtained

* Note.   at   °, between the hours of
Insert   and   on
description
of place   Every nomination paper must be signed by
and room.   two registered electors as proposer and seconder,
and by eight other registered electors as assenting to the nomination.

Every nomination paper must be delivered to the returning officer by the candidate proposed, or by his proposer and seconder, between the said hours of
and   on the said   day of
at the said   °.

Each candidate nominated, and his proposer and seconder,
and one other person selected by the candidate, and no
other persons, are entitled to be admitted to the room.

In the event of the election being contested, the poll
will take place on the   day of

(Signed)   A.B.,
Sheriff [or Mayor, or as the case may be].
day of   18 .

Take notice, that all persons who are guilty of bribery,
treating, undue influence, personation, or other corrupt
practices at the said election will, on conviction of such

offence, be liable to the penalties mentioned in that behalf in " The Corrupt Practices Prevention Act, 1854," and the Ballot Act, 1872, and the Acts amending the said Acts.

The Act which now prescribes the penalties for the above offences, and other offences created by it, is the Corrupt Practices Act, 1883.

Form of Nomination Paper in Parliamentary Election.

We, the undersigned *A.B.* of   in the of   and *C.D.* of   in the   of   , being electors for the   of   , do hereby nominate the following person as a proper person to serve as member for the said   in Parliament :

Surname.	Other Names.	Abode.	Rank, Profession, or Occupation.
BROWN	JOHN	52, George St., Bristol	Merchant.
JONES	*or* WILLIAM DAVID ...	High Elms, Wilts	Esquire.
MERTON	*or* Hon. GEORGE TRAVIS, commonly called Viscount	Swanworth, Berks	Viscount.
SMITH	*or* HENRY SYDNEY ...	72, High St., Bath	Attorney.

(Signed)   *A.B.*
    C.D.

We, the undersigned, being registered electors of the
do hereby assent to the nomination of the
above-mentioned *John Brown* as a proper person to serve
as member for the said   in Parliament.

(Signed)   *E.F.* of
             G.H. of
             I.J. of
             K.L. of
             M.N. of
             O.P. of
             Q.R. of
             S.T. of

Note.—Where a candidate is an Irish peer, or is commonly
known by some title, he may be described by his title as if
it were his surname.

Form of Nomination Paper in Municipal Election.

Note.—The form of nomination paper in a municipal or county council election shall as nearly as circumstances admit be the same as in the case of a parliamentary election.

Form of Ballot Paper.

Form of Front of Ballot Paper.

Counterfoil No.			
NOTE: *The counter-foil is to have a number to correspond with that on the back of the Ballot Paper.*	1	**BROWN** (John Brown, of 52, George Street, Bristol, merchant.)	
	2	**JONES** (William David Jones, of High Elms, Wilts, Esq.)	
	3	**MERTON** (Hon. George Travis, commonly called Viscount Merton, of Swanworth, Berks.)	
	4	**SMITH** (Henry Sydney Smith, of 72, High Street, Bath, Attorney.)	

Form of Back of Ballot Paper.

No.   Election for   county [or
                  borough, *or* ward].   18 .

Note.—The number on the ballot paper is to correspond with that in the counterfoil.

Direction as to printing Ballot Paper.

Nothing is to be printed on the ballot paper except in accordance with this schedule.

The surname of each candidate, and if there are two or more candidates of the same surname, also the other names of such candidates, shall be printed in large characters, as shown in the form, and the names, addresses, and descriptions, and the number on the back of the paper, shall be printed in small characters.

Form of Directions for the Guidance of the Voter in voting, which shall be printed in conspicuous characters, and placarded outside every Polling Station and in every compartment of every Polling Station.

The voter may vote for   candidate .

The voter will go into one of the compartments, and, with the pencil provided in the compartment, place a cross on the right-hand side, opposite the name of each candidate for whom he votes, thus X

The voter will then fold up the ballot paper so as to show the official mark on the back, and leaving the compartment will, without showing the front of the paper to any person, show the official mark on the back to the presiding officer, and then, in the presence of the presiding officer, put the paper into the ballot box, and forthwith quit the polling station.

If the voter inadvertently spoils a ballot paper, he can return it to the officer, who will, if satisfied of such inadvertence, give him another paper.

If the voter votes for more than   candidate , or places any mark on the paper by which he may be afterwards identified, his ballot paper will be void, and will not be counted.

If the voter takes a ballot paper out of the polling station, or deposits in the ballot box any other paper than the one given him by the officer, he will be guilty of a misdemeanour, and be subject to imprisonment for any term not exceeding six months, with or without hard labour.

Note.—These directions shall be illustrated by examples of the ballot paper.

Form of Statutory Declaration of Secrecy.

I solemnly promise and declare, That I will not at this election for   do anything forbidden by section four of The Ballot Act, 1872, which has been read to me.

Note.—The section must be read to the declarant by the person taking the declaration.

Form of Declaration of inability to read.

I, *A.B.*, of   , being numbered
on the Register of Voters for the County [*or* Borough]
of   do hereby declare that I am unable to read.

                                   A.B.,   his mark.
          day of
I, the undersigned, being the presiding officer for the
          polling station for the county [*or* borough]
of   , do hereby certify, that the above declaration, having been first read to the above-named *A.B.*, was signed by him in my presence with his mark.

          (Signed)   *C.*
Presiding officer for   polling station for the
          county [*or* borough] of
          day of

THE EFFECT UPON THE ELECTION OF BREACHES OF THE PROVISIONS OF THE BALLOT ACT.

The Ballot Act, which has created an elaborate machinery for the taking of votes at a contested election, lays down in the schedule to the Act very precise directions as to the method in which those charged with its conduct are to conduct every detail. A practical question of the first importance is—What is the effect upon the validity of an election of a breach of all, or any, of these directions ? On the one hand it would be unjust that the failure of the returning officer strictly to adhere to every one of the rules should invalidate the election. On the other hand it would be of dangerous consequence if an election conducted in open breach of all the provisions of the Legislature should stand. In every case the difficulty is to distinguish between the mere irregularity which may expose the person guilty of it to an action or some penalty, but which does not affect the election, and that fundamental departure from the principles of the Ballot Act which destroys the return.

This distinction is accentuated by section 13 of the Ballot Act, which, while it is careful to declare that an election shall not be vacated by any informality or for any non-compliance with the directions contained in the Schedule, clearly implies that the return is invalid where the election has been conducted in defiance of the principles laid down in the body of the Act, and the result has been affected thereby. And it must now be taken to be clear law, that where in the carrying out of the election (a) the principles of the Ballot Act have been violated and (b) the result has been affected thereby, the election will be set aside (The HACKNEY CASE, 2 O'M. & H., 77 ; The DROGHEDA CASE, 2 O'M. & H., 201; WOODWARD v. SARSONS, 10 C. P., 746).

What are the principles of the Ballot Act? They are no where in so many words defined in the Act, "and nothing can be more difficult than for a judge or for a metaphysician or for anybody to say what are the principles of a statute which consists, together with the schedules, of upwards of 100 pages," (Per Grove, J., in the HACKNEY CASE *supra*). In the same case, however, the learned judge went on to define at least two principles of the Ballot Act. One principle he held was, that the *voting should be secret*, and another principle that the electors should have *a fair opportunity of recording their votes*. There may be other principles of the Act, but the cases in which an election has been sought to be upset for non-compliance with some principle of the Act may be referred to one or other of these heads.

There is no reported case where an election has been invalidated because it was conducted under circumstances that imperilled or destroyed the secrecy of the voting, though, in several instances, objection has been taken to the return on that ground. The leading case is the DROGHEDA CASE, (2 O'M. & H., 201). There four of the seven polling stations were held in private houses, and each polling station consisted of two rooms on the first or drawing room floor, immediately adjoining one another *but with no internal communication*. The presiding officer and his clerks sat in one room, and into that room the voter, in the first instance, passed from the landing at the top of the stairs, and there received his voting paper. He then returned to the landing as the only means of getting into the second room, and arrived there, he marked his paper. Having marked the paper he was compelled to return by way of the landing to the first room where he deposited his paper in the ballot box. A policeman was stationed on the landing to prevent any person interfering with voters while passing from one room to the other, but there was nothing to prevent a voter, if so minded, showing his paper after it was marked to anyone who might be coming upstairs. There was no evidence that this was in fact done, nor was there any evidence that the result of the election was affected. It was also proved that the high sheriff, the sub-sheriff, the resident magistrate in charge of the polling, and the policemen had not taken the declaration of secrecy prescribed by the Act, and there was evidence that these persons had accidentally heard how several illiterates voted. Barry, J., who tried the case, referred the question of whether under the circumstances the election should be declared void to the Court of Common Pleas. In the event the Judges there were equally divided, and the case coming back to Barry, J., he ultimately decided in favour of the validity of the election.

In the BOLTON CASE (2 O'M. & H., 138), the respondent's agents in the polling stations, in violation of sec. 4 of the Ballot Act, communicated to persons outside the names of the voters who had applied for ballot papers. Mellor, J., held that though a deliberate violation of the provision with regard to the secrecy of voting had been attempted, he could not on that ground alone declare the election invalid.

In WOODWARD v. SARSONS (10 C. P., 746), the presiding officer, before delivering the ballot papers to the electors, marked upon the face of a large number of them the number of the voter appearing on the burgess roll in a manner which would have enabled any person present at the counting to identify the way in which the party voted. It was held that this error of the presiding officer, which had no effect on the result, did not render the election void.

It must be observed with regard to all the cases quoted above that in no instance was the court satisfied that the result of the election had been affected by the irregularities complained of. They must not, therefore, be taken as authorities for the proposition that under no circumstances would an election conducted in the manner in which they were conducted be set aside.

The second principle of the Ballot Act, mentioned by Grove, J., is that the electors shall have a fair opportunity of recording their votes. It was on a suggestion that such opportunity had not been accorded that objection was taken to the return in the HACKNEY CASE (2 O'M. & H., 77). There it was proved that in a borough with 41,000 electors, two polling stations at which 4,838 voters were entitled to vote were never opened at all, and that three other polling places at which 3,938 voters were entitled to vote were only open during part of the day. Grove, J., held that the principle of the Ballot Act, which required that the electors should have a fair opportunity of giving their votes, had been violated, and that the irregularities complained of had more or less affected the result, and he declared the election void.

In the DROGHEDA CASE (2 O'M. & H., 201), it was shown that the polling stations were not opened until a quarter to nine instead of at eight, but the learned judge found as a fact that this irregularity did not have the remotest effect upon the result of the voting, and he upheld the election. In the WORCESTER CASE (3 O'M. & H., 184), objection was taken to the return on the ground that two polling stations were closed a little before four and while voters were waiting to vote, but no decision was given upon the legal effect of closing the poll a quarter of an hour before the authorised time, because the court held that in fact the poll was kept open until four. It is apprehended that the premature closing of the poll would have had no effect upon the return unless the court was satisfied that the result either was or might have been affected by what had happened.

In the HACKNEY CASE, Grove, J. made some important remarks upon the meaning of the words, " the result of the election," in the 13th section of the Ballot Act, which it may be well to reproduce here. "I am very strongly inclined to think," said his lordship, "that the expression, ' the result of the election,' does not in this Act necessarily mean the result as to another candidate having been elected at the poll. The result may be of various kinds. The result of the election would, in my judgment, be affected, if instead of a majority of 500, there was a majority of only 10 or even 100. Upon a scrutiny the matter might be very different. Other causes might also produce a very considerable change of relation between the parties, and might have a very important effect upon the ultimate, if not upon the then present representation in Parliament, that effect depending upon the magnitude of the majority. It will also be observed that the words used in the section are not ' did not *alter* the result of the election,' but ' did not *affect* the result of the election.' Does not the word ' affect ' mean substantially ' bear upon the result ? ' " (2 O'M. & H., 84).

REFERENCES TO THE ACTS WHICH PRESCRIBE THE PROCEDURE, &c., AT PARLIAMENTARY, MUNICIPAL & COUNTY COUNCIL ELECTIONS.

☞ *E—means that the Statute applies only to England ; S—Scotland ; I—Ireland.*

Elections to be free—3 Edw. 1 (Stat. West. Prim.) c. 5. 1 Will. & Mary, sess. 2, c. 2.

AS TO ISSUE AND DELIVERY OF WRITS TO RETURNING OFFICERS :—

Forty days between *teste* and return of writs of summons—7 & 8 Will. 3, c. 25, s. 1.

Writs to be issued with expedition—7 & 8 Will. 3, c. 25, s. 1.

Issue of writs for elections in counties of Lancaster and Durham, and boroughs therein—(E.) 30 & 31 Vict. c. 102, s. 57.   (E.) 31 & 32 Vict. c. 58, s. 21.

Writs to be made conformable to Acts—(E.) 2 & 3 Will. 4, c. 45, s. 77.   (E.) 16 & 17 Vict. c. 68, s. 1, (E.) 24 & 25 Vict. c. 112, s. 14.   (E.) 30 & 31 Vict. c. 102. s. 58.

Form of Writ—35 & 36 Vict. c. 33, s. 28.   Sch. 2.

Notice of issue of writs to be given to Secretary of State for War department, and by him to generals in districts —10 & 11 Vict. c. 21, s. 2.   26 & 27 Vict. c. 12.

Writ to be delivered to officer to whom execution belongs. who shall take no fee for execution—7 & 8 Will. 3, c. 25. ss. 1, 2, 5.

AS TO RETURNING OFFICERS :—

In counties, divisions of counties, and counties of cities, sheriffs of counties, and sheriffs of counties of cities, to be—7 & 8 Will. 3, c. 25. (E.) 2 & 3 Will. 4, c. 45, s. 61. (E.) 16 & 17 Vict. c. 68, s. 1. (E.) 30 & 31 Vict. c. 102, s. 23.

Appointment by sheriffs in divided counties of deputies for election purposes ; deputies or under sheriffs acting, to be deemed returning officers—(E.) 2 & 3 Will. 4, c. 45, s. 61. (E.) 30 & 31 Vict. c. 102, s. 23. (E.) 35 & 36 Vict. c. 33, s. 8.

In Isle of Wight sheriff or deputy to be—(E.) 2 & 3 Will. 4, c. 45, s. 16.

Appointment of certain officers to be returning officers in certain cities and boroughs—(E.) 2 & 3 Will. 4, c. 45, ss. 10, 11. Schs. C. D.

Appointment by sheriff and qualification of returning officers in other boroughs—(E.) 2 & 3 Will. 4, c. 45, s. 11. Schs. C. D. (E.) 30 & 31 Vict. c. 102, s. 47. Schs. B. C.

In Thirsk—(E.) 31 & 32 Vict. c. 58, s. 27.

Mayor, or alderman elected in his place, or deputy mayor to be returning officer where borough is a municipal borough—(E.) 2 & 3 Will. 4, c. 45, s. 11. Schs. C. D. (E.) 5 & 6 Will. 4, c. 76, s. 57. (E.) 16 & 17 Vict. c. 79, ss. 7, 8. (E.) 30 & 31 Vict. c. 102, s. 47. · Schs. B. C. (E.) 31 & 32 Vict. c. 58, s. 33.

In Brighton—(E.) 18 & 19 Vict. c. 31, s. 2.

In Coventry—(E.) 5 & 6 Vict. c. 110, s. 10.

Sheriff of county to act as returning officer in borough where there is no person qualified—(E.) 17 & 18 Vict. c. 57.

AS TO WRITS (HOW TO BE DIRECTED, &c.) :—

For counties and divisions of counties to sheriffs of counties—(E.) 16 & 17 Vict. c. 68, s. 1.

For counties of cities to sheriffs thereof—(E.) 16 & 17 Vict. c. 68, s. 1.

For cities and boroughs to returning officers or their deputies, or in their absence to sheriffs of counties—

(E.) 16 & 17 Vict. c. 68, s. 1. (E.) 17 & 18 Vict. c. 57.

For Cheshire to sheriff of county—(E.) 9 & 10 Vict. c. 44.

For Chester to sheriff of county of city—(E.) 9 & 10 Vict. c. 44.

For counties of Lancaster and Durham, and boroughs therein, as writs for other counties and boroughs— (E.) 30 & 31 Vict. c. 102, s. 57. (E.) 31 & 32 Vict. c. 58, s. 21.

Writs addressed to sheriffs of London and Middlesex, or to returning officers having offices in or near London, Westminster or Southwark to be delivered ; all others to be sent through the post; fees on conveyance of writs abolished—(E.S.) 53 Geo. 3, c. 89. (E.) 31 & 32 Vict. c. 102, s. 57. (E.) 31 & 32 Vict. c. 58, s. 21. (E.S.) 37 & 38 Vict. c. 81, s. 4.

Indorsement on writ of day of receipt—7 & 8 Will. 3, c. 25, s. 1. 35 & 36 Vict. c. 33, s. 28. Sch. 2.

AS TO ELECTION AND RETURN :—

Returning officer on receipt of writ to proceed to election—(E.) 16 & 17 Vict. c. 68, s. 1.

Notice of election, and of time and place, and of day for poll in case of contest—(E.) 2 & 3 Will. 4, c. 45, s. 61. 35 & 36 Vict. c. 33, ss. 15, 17, 28. Sch. 1, rule 1. Sch. 2.

Day for election, and time and place of election—35 & 36 Vict. c. 33, ss. 16, 17, 28. Sch. 1, rules 2, 4, 58.

Nomination of candidates—35 & 36 Vict. c. 33, ss. 1, 8, 16, 17, 28. Sch. 1, rules 5, 8, 10, 13. Sch. 2.

Nomination not to be made at place of worship—(E.) 2 & 3 Will. 4, c. 45, s. 68.

Adjournment of nomination in case of riot—(E.) 5 & 6 Will. 4, c. 36, s. 8.

Candidates nominated, if no more than number of vacancies, to be elected and names returned—35 & 36 Vict. c. 33, ss. 1, 16, 17.

If more candidates than vacancies, election to be adjourned and poll taken—35 & 36 Vict. c. 33, ss. 1, 16, 17, 28. Sch. 1, rules 10-13.

Withdrawal of candidate before adjournment—35 & 36 Vict. c. 33, ss. 1, 16, 17, 28. Sch. 1, rule 10.

Withdrawal of candidate not finding security for expenses—(E.I.) 38 & 39 Vict. c. 84, s. 3. (S.) 41 & 42 Vict. c. 41, s. 3.

Proceedings to recommence on death of candidate, after adjournment and before poll—35 & 36 Vict. c. 33, ss. 1, 16, 17.

Poll to be taken by ballot—35 & 36 Vict. c. 33, ss. 2, 16, 17.

Division of counties and boroughs into polling districts and appointment of polling places—(E.) 30 & 31 Vict. c. 102, s. 34. (E.) 31 & 32 Vict. c. 48, s. 18. (E.) 35 & 36 Vict. c. 33, s. 5. (E.) 46 & 47 Vict. c. 51, s. 47.

Poll not to be taken at place of worship—(E.) 2 & 3 Will. 4, c. 45, s. 68 ;

Nor, except by consent of candidates, at public-house— (E.) 16 & 17 Vict. c. 68, s. 6.

Hire of buildings or rooms, and use of school or public room for poll—(E.) 30 & 31 Vict. c. 102, s. 37. 35 & 36 Vict. c. 33, ss. 6, 16, 17.

Erection of booths, providing of polling stations, ballot boxes, papers, copies of registers, &c., voters to vote only at booths or stations allotted—(E.) 2 & 3 Will. 4, c. 45, ss. 64, 68, 71. 35 & 36 Vict. c. 33, ss. 2, 8, 15, 17, 28. Sch. 1, rules 15-20, 22, 23. Sch. 2.

Use of ballot-boxes, stations, &c., provided for municipal or school board elections for Parliamentary elections, and *vice versa*.—35 & 36 Vict. c. 33, ss. 14, 16, 17. (E. I.) 38 & 39 Vict. c. 84, s. 6. (S.) 41 & 42 Vict. c. 41, s. 4.

Liverymen of City of London, where to vote—(E.) 5 & 6 Will. 4, c. 36, s. 7. (E.) 6 & 7 Vict. c. 18, s. 92.

Appointment and powers of presiding officers and clerks—35 & 36 Vict. c. 33, ss. 8-10, 16, 17, 28. Sch. 1, rules 21, 47-50, 63.

Providing of constables at polling stations—(E.) 6 & 7 Vict. c. 18, s. 90.

Appointment by candidates of personation agents, and agents to attend counting of votes ; powers of agents.—(E.) 6 & 7 Vict. c. 18, s. 85. 35 & 36 Vict. c. 33, ss. 15-17, 28. Sch. 1, rules 21, 31-37, 52-55, 59.

Declaration of secrecy by returning officer, officers and agents.—35 & 36 Vict. c. 33, ss. 16, 17, 28. Sch. 1, rule 54. Sch. 2.

Poll, day for, commencement and continuance of—

In counties.—(E.) 16 & 17 Vict. c. 15, s. 2. 35 & 36 Vict. c. 33, ss. 16, 17, 28. Sch. 1, rules 14, 61.

In boroughs.—(E.) 5 & 6 Will. 4, c. 36, s. 2. 35 & 36 Vict. c. 33, ss. 16, 17, 28. Sch. 1, rules 14, 61.

Duration of.—48 & 49 Vict. c. 10.

Voting at poll, administration of oaths to voters, grounds on which votes may be rejected.—(E.) 6 & 7 Vict. c. 18. ss. 81, 82. 35 & 36 Vict. c. 33, ss. 2, 10, 15-17, 28. Sch. 1, rules 24-28. Sch. 2.

Number of votes where three members returned.—30 & 31 Vict. c. 102, s. 9.

Number of votes in City of London.—30 & 31 Vict. c. 102, s. 10.

Production of books of admission of freemen.—(E.) 3 Geo. 3, c. 15, ss 4-8.

Keeping order in polling stations —35 & 36 Vict. c. 33, ss. 9, 10, 16, 17, 28. Sch. 1, rule 21.

Adjournment of poll in case of riot.—(E.) 2 & 3 Will. 4, c 45, s. 70. (E.) 5 & 6 Will. 4, c. 36, s. 8. (E.) 16 & 17 Vict. c. 15, s. 3. 35 & 36 Vict. c. 33, ss. 10, 15, 17.

Close of poll, return of ballot-boxes, &c., to returning officer, counting of votes, objections to votes, and decision thereon.—35 & 36 Vict. c. 33, ss. 2, 16, 17, 28. Sch. 1, rules 29-37, 48.

Returning officer, if registered, to have casting vote, but no other vote.—35 & 36 Vict. c. 33, ss. 2, 16, 17.

Declaration of result of election, return of result by post to Clerk of the Crown, or Clerk of the Crown and Hanaper in Ireland, by indorsement on writ.—35 & 36 Vict c. 33, ss. 1, 2, 16, 17, 28. Sch. 1, rules 44, 63. Sch. 2.

Report to Clerk of the Crown, Sheriff Clerk in Scotland, and Clerk of the Crown and Hanaper in Ireland, as to votes rejected, &c., return of ballot papers, &c., by post to Clerk of the Crown, &c., custody and production thereof.—(E.) 6 & 7 Vict. c. 18, ss. 93, 97.

35 & 36 Vict. c. 33, ss. 16, 17, 28. Sch. 1, rules 36-43, 59, 63.

Clerk of the Crown to enter returns and alterations therein, allow inspection, and give copies; penalty for neglect, giving false certificate, or altering return except by order of the House.—7 & 8 Will. 3, c. 7, ss. 5, 6.

Penalty on sheriff omitting return to writ.—5 Ric. 2, st. 2, c. 4.

Prohibition of and damages for false returns, returns contrary to last determination of House, of right of election, false.—7 & 8 Will. 3, c. 7, ss. 1, 2.

Contracts to secure returns, void; penalty for entering into such contracts.—7 & 8 Will. 3, c. 7, ss. 4, 6.

AS TO ELECTIONS FOR UNIVERSITIES :—

How far exempt from general enactments.—(E.) 2 & 3 Will. 4. c. 45, s. 78. (E.) 30 & 31 Vict. c. 102, s. 2. 35 & 36 Vict. c. 33, ss. 27, 31. (E. I.) 38 & 39 Vict. c. 84, s. 8.

Issue and delivery of writ, form of writ and indorsement on writ. (See above.)

Writs to be addressed to Vice-Chancellors as Returning Officers who shall proceed to election and certify result.

Oxford and Cambridge.—(E.) 25 Geo. 3, c. 84 s. 1. (E.) 16 & 17 Vict. c. 68, s. 1.

London.—(E.) 30 & 31 Vict. c. 102, ss. 40, 41.

Notice of time and place of election.

Oxford and Cambridge.—(E.) 33 Geo. 3, c. 64.

London.—(E.) 30 & 31 Vict. c. 102, s. 42.

Appointment of polling places, Pro Vice-Chancellors and officers.

Oxford and Cambridge.—(E.) 16 & 17 Vict. c. 68, s. 5.

London.—(E.) 30 & 31 Vict. c. 102, s. 44.

Commencement and hours of poll and continuance for five days.

Oxford and Cambridge.—(E.) 25 Geo. 3, c. 84, ss. 1, 3. (E.) 16 & 17 Vict. c. 68, s. 4.

London.—(E.) 30 & 31 Vict. c. 102, s. 43.

Voting by voting papers and offences as to voting papers.

Oxford, Cambridge and Dublin.—(E. I.) 24 & 25 Vict. c. 53.   (E. I.) 31 & 32 Vict. c. 65.

London.—(E.) 30 & 31 Vict. c. 102, s. 45. (E.) 31 & 32 Vict. c. 65.

Declaration of election and return.

Oxford and Cambridge.—(E.) 25 Geo. 3, c. 84, s. 1. (E.) 16 & 17 Vict. c. 68, s. 1.

London.—(E.) 30 & 31 Vict. c. 102, ss. 42, 44.

As to the manner of election and voting for Scotch Universities see 31 & 32 Vict. c. 48, as amended by 44 & 45 Vict. c. 40.

AS TO EXPENSES OF ELECTIONS :—

(1.) *Of Candidates.*

Definition of candidate.—46 & 47 Vict. c. 51, s. 63.

Personal expenses.—17 & 18 Vict. c. 102, s. 38.   46 & 47 Vict. c. 51, ss. 31, 66.

Expenses, other than personal expenses, to be paid only through agents.—46 & 47 Vict. c. 51, ss. 28, 29.

Appointment of agents, and publication of names and addresses.—46 & 47 Vict. c. 51, s. 24.

Return of, to be, transmitted to returning officer—46 & 47 Vict. c. 51, s. 33.

Disputed claims may be taxed.—46 & 47 Vict. c. 51, s. 30.

Limitation of time for recovery of claims.—46 & 47 Vict. c. 51, s. 29.

Publication of statement of expenses.—46 & 47 Vict. c. 51, ss. 33, 35.

(2.) *Of Returning Officers.*

Account of expenses of, to be transmitted to election agents.—46 & 47 Vict. c. 51, s. 32.

Payments to returning officers for services and expenses.—(E. I.) 38 & 39 Vict. c. 84, s. 2.   Sch. 46 & 47 Vict. c. 51.   Sch. 1. (E.)   48 & 49 Vict. c. 62, s. 4.

Expenses to be paid by candidates through election agent, persons nominating a candidate without his

consent to be liable for his share.—(E.) 2 & 3 Will.
4, c. 45, s. 71. (E. I.) 35 & 36 Vict. c. 33, ss. 8,
17. (E. I.) 38 & 39 Vict. c. 84, s. 2. 46 & 47 Vict.
c. 51, s. 28.

Security for expenses.—(E. I.) 38 & 39 Vict. c. 84,
s. 3. 48 & 49 Vict. c. 62. (S.) 41 & 42 Vict. c. 41,
s. 3. Sch.

Accounts ; taxation and enforcement of payment by
Lord Mayor's Court, County Court, or Civil Bill
Court.—(E. I.) 38 & 39 Vict. c. 84, ss. 4. 6.

Limitation of time for recovery of claims against returning officers ; notice to be given.—(E. I.) 38 &
39 Vict. c. 84, ss. 5, 7. Sch. 2.

Acts not to apply to elections for Universities.—2 &
3 Will. 4, c. 45, s. 78. 35 & 36 Vict. c. 33, s. 31.
(E. I.) 38 & 39 Vict. c. 84, s. 8. (S.) 41 & 42
Vict. c. 41, s. 5.

Act applying to all constituencies.—46 & 47 Vict. c. 51.

AS TO OFFENCES AT ELECTIONS : PENALTIES :—

Offences as to nomination papers, ballot papers, and
ballot boxes.—35 & 36 Vict. c. 33, ss. 3, 16, 17.

Infringement of secrecy by officers, clerks, agents, &c.
—35 & 36 Vict. c. 33, ss. 4. 16, 17.

Personation ; proceedings on charge of, at time of
voting ; prosecution for, by returning officer, and
penalty for.—(E.) 6 & 7 Vict. c. 18, ss. 85, 89. 35 &
36 Vict. c. 33, ss. 24-27. 46 & 47 Vict. c. 51, s. 6.

Penalties on commission of any other corrupt, illegal
or unlawful practice or act.—46 & 47 Vict. c. 51,
ss. 6, 10, 21 & 36.

Penalties on returning officers, postmasters, and other
officers, for misconduct or neglect of duty.—5 Ric. 2,
st. 2, c. 4. 7 & 8 Will. 3, c. 7. 7 & 8 Will. 3, c. 25.
(E.) 2 & 3 Will. 4, c. 45, s. 76. (E.) 6 & 7 Vict. c.
18, s. 97. 35 & 36 Vict. c. 33, ss. 11, 16, 17. 46 & 47
Vict. c. 51, s. 61.

Action against returning officer for not returning person
held entitled, on trial on election petition, to have been
returned.—31 & 32 Vict. c. 125, ss. 48, 58.

Relief against illegal practice or unlawful act.—46 & 47 Vict. c. 51, ss. 23, 24.

MISCELLANEOUS PROVISIONS :—

Canvassing at elections prohibited—
  by Commissioners, &c., of Metropolitan Police at certain elections.—(E.) 10 Geo. 4, c. 44, s. 18. (E.) 19 & 20 Vict. c. 2, s. 9. (E.) 23 & 24 Vict. c. 135, s. 5.
  by county police at certain elections.—(E.) 2 & 3 Vict. c. 93, s. 9.
  by borough police at certain elections.—(E.) 19 & 20 Vict. c. 69, s. 9.
Soldiers to remain in barracks during elections.—10 & 11 Vict. c. 21.   26 & 27 Vict. c. 12.
Power of sheriff or deputy to act in places of exclusive jurisdiction.—(E.) 2 & 3 Will. 4, c. 45, s. 66. (E.) 2 & 3 Will. 4, c. 64, s. 28.
Marking of boundaries of boroughs by returning officers. —(E.) 31 & 32 Vict. c. 46, s. 12.
Jurisdiction of returning officers on alteration of boundaries.—(E.) 31 & 32 Vict. c. 58, s. 35.
Returning officers and deputies, presiding and other officers and their partners or clerks, not to act as agents for candidates.—(E.) 30 & 31 Vict. c. 102, s. 50. 35 & 36 Vict. c. 33, ss. 11, 16, 17.
Voter not to be required to state for whom he voted.— 35 & 36 Vict. c. 33, ss. 12, 16, 17.
Election not to be questioned for non-compliance or informality as to polling districts or places.—(E.) 35 & 36 Vict. c. 33, s. 5.
Elections not to be invalidated by non-compliance with rules, or mistake as to forms.—35 & 36 Vict. c. 33, ss. 13, 16, 17.
Saving and application of election laws.—(E.) 2 & 3 Will. 4, c. 45, s. 75. (E.) 30 & 31 Vict. c. 102, s. 56. 35 & 36 Vict. c. 33, ss. 15-17.

AS TO ELECTION PETITIONS :—

Election or return to be questioned only by petition.— 31 & 32 Vict. c. 125, ss. 50, 58.

Definition and jurisdiction of court; prescribed officer.
—(E. I.) 31 & 32 Vict. c. 125, ss. 21, 27. (E.) 36 & 37
Vict. c. 66, ss. 3, 16, 31, 34. (I.) 40 & 41 Vict. c. 57,
ss. 3, 21, 34, 36.

Presentment of petition to Court, who may present;
security for costs; form and service of petition;
respondents; presentation of more that one petition.—
(E. I.) 31 & 32 Vict. c. 125, ss. 5, 6, 20-23.

Copy to be sent to and published by returning officer.—
(E. I.) 31 & 32 Vict. c. 125, s. 7.

Notice to respondent; objections to security; determination of objections; publication of list of petitions.
—(E. I.) 31 & 32 Vict. c. 125, ss. 8, 10.

Withdrawal or abatement of petition; substitution of
petitioner; corrupt agreement for withdrawal.—(E. I.)
31 & 32 Vict. c. 125, ss. 35, 37. 46 & 47 Vict. c. 51,
ss. 41, 66.

Admission of voters as respondents in certain cases.—
(E. I.) 31 & 32 Vict. c. 125, s. 38.

Respondent not opposing not to appear as a party or to
sit or vote in Parliament pending decision.—(E. I.)
31 & 32 Vict. c. 125, s. 39.

Withdrawal of petition and certificate to Speaker where
petition against one member only on double return is
not opposed.—(E. I.) 31 & 32 Vict. c. 125, s. 40.

Returning officer complained of may be made respondent.
—(E. I.) 31 & 32 Vict. c. 125, s. 51.

Petition complaining of no return.—(E. I.) 31 & 32 Vict.
c. 125, s. 52.

Time within which petition to be presented.—31 & 32
Vict. c. 125 s. 6. 46 & 47 Vict. c. 51, s. 40.

Trial of petition by judges selected from rota; place and
time of trial, adjournment, reception of and attendance
on judges; expenses; powers of judges.—(E. I.)
31 & 32 Vict. c. 125, ss. 11, 28—30, 55. (E.) 36 & 37
Vict. c. 66, s. 38. (I.) 40 & 41 Vict. c. 57, s. 43.
42 & 43 Vict. c. 75 s. 2. 46 & 47 Vict. c. 51, s. 42.

Two judges instead of one to preside at trial.—42 & 43
Vict. c. 75, s. 2.

Reservation of questions of law; trial of petition as
special case by court.—(E. I.) 31 & 32 Vict. c. 125,
ss. 11, 12.

Attendance of shorthand writer of House.—(E. I.)
31 & 32 Vict. c. 125, s. 24.

Trial not stopped by acceptance of office or prorogation
of Parliament.—(E. I.) 31 & 32 Vict. c. 125,
ss. 18, 19.

Evidence of corrupt practices, how received.—(E. I.)
31 & 32 Vict. c. 125, s. 17. 46 & 47 Vict. c. 51, s. 43.

Rules for procedure, &c.; application of practice of
election committees.—(E. I.) 31 & 32 Vict. c. 125,
ss. 25, 26.

Agents entitled to practise before election committees
entitled to practise on petitions.—(E. I.) 31 & 32 Vict.
c. 125, s. 57.

Witnesses, summoning, examination, indemnity, and expenses of.—(E. I.) 31 & 32 Vict. c. 125, ss. 31, 32, 34.

Costs and forfeiture of recognizances.—(E. I.) 31 & 32
Vict. c. 125, ss. 41, 42, 46 & 47 Vict. c. 51 s. 44.

Recrimination on petition complaining of undue return
and claiming seat.—(E. I.) 31 & 32 Vict. c. 125, s. 53.

Striking off of votes on scrutiny, on trial of petition
claiming seat, on proof of corrupt practices, or of
voting by agents, &c.—35 & 36 Vict. c. 33, ss. 25—27.

Decision by judges or court; certificate to Speaker;
report as to corrupt practices, &c.—(E. I.) 31 & 32
Vict. c. 125, ss. 11, 12. 42 & 43 Vict. c. 75, s. 2.

Certificate to be final; House to give effect to certificate, and report by alteration of return, issue of
new writ, &c.—(E. I.) 31 & 32 Vict. c. 125, ss. 13,
14, 40.

Application of Parliamentary Elections Act to Scotland.
—(S.) 31 & 32 Vict. c. 125, s. 58.

ELECTION OF MUNICIPAL OR COUNTY COUN-
CILLORS :—

Councillors, election for borough or ward.—45 & 46 Vict.
c. 50, s. 50.

Councillors, title to vote at election.—45 & 46 Vict. c. 50,
ss. 51, 58 (2).

Councillors, day of election, and notice.—45 & 46 Vict.
c. 50, ss. 52, 54.

Councillors, returning officer.—45 & 46 Vict. c. 50,
s. 53 ; 51 & 52 Vict. c. 41, s. 75.

Councillors, nomination and withdrawal of candidate. —45 & 46 Vict. c. 50, s. 55, sch. 3, part II., 8, part II.

Councillors, relation of nomination to election.—45 & 46 Vict. c. 50, s. 56.

Councillors, publication of uncontested election.—45 & 46 Vict. c. 50, s. 57.

Councillor, mode of conducting poll at contested election by ballot.—45 & 46 Vict. c. 50, s. 58 (1), sch. 3, parts III., IV., 8, part II.

Councillors, hours of polling from 8 a.m. to 8 p.m.—45 & 46 Vict. c. 50, s. 58 (3), (4). 48 & 49 Vict. c. 10.

Councillors, casting vote of returning officer.—45 & 46 Vict. c. 50, s. 58 (5).

Councillors, provisions as to agents of candidate.—45 & 46 Vict. c. 50, s. 58 (6).

Councillors, questions to voters.—45 & 46 Vict. c. 50, s. 59.

Councillors, election of, in more than one ward.—45 & 46 Vict. c. 50, s. 68.

Procedure for division of borough into wards, or alteration of wards : remuneration of commissioner.—45 & 46 Vict. c. 50, s. 30, sch. 4 and 5.

Division of borough or ward into polling districts.—45 & 46 Vict c. 50, s. 64.

Supplemental provisions as to notices.—45 & 46 Vict. c. 50, s. 65.

Illness or incapacity of returning officer.—45 & 46 Vict. c. 50. s. 67.

Election not in place of worship.—45 & 46 Vict. c. 50, s. 69.

Provisions if election not held, or void.—45 & 46 Vict. c 50, s. 70.

Election not invalid for irregularity.—45 & 46 Vict. c. 50, s. 72.

Election valid, unless questioned within 12 months.—45 & 46 Vict. c. 50, s. 73.

Use of ballot boxes, &c., provided for parliamentary elections.—35 & 36 Vict. c 33 (1), s. 14.

Jurisdiction of county court as to election documents after return.—35 & 36 Vict. c. 33 (1), sch. 1, part II.

CORRUPT PRACTICES AND ELECTION PETITIONS :—

Security for costs by petitioner.—45 & 46 Vict. c. 50, s. 89.

List of petitions at issue : order of trial.—45 & 46 Vict. c. 50, ss. 90, 91.

Constitution powers, expenses of election court, including expenses of Director of Public Prosecutions.—45 & 46 Vict. c. 50, ss. 92, 99, 101. 47 & 48 Vict. c. 70 (I) s. 28 (8) (9).

Time and place of trial, certificate as to election and report as to corrupt practices, &c., to High Court, special case for High Court.—45 & 46 Vict. c. 50, s. 93. 47 & 48 Vict. c. 70 (1). s. 27

Decision of High Court final, unless special leave to appeal.—44 & 45 Vict. c. 68, s. 14.

Witnesses, summoning, &c., of ; certificate to.—45 & 46 Vict. c. 50, s. 94. 47 & 48 Vict. c. 70 (1), s. 38, sch. 2.

Withdrawal of petition ; abatement by death of petitioner.—45 & 46 Vict. c. 50, ss. 95-97.

Withdrawal of petition ; further restrictions on withdrawal.—47 & 48 Vict. c. 70 (1), s 26.

Costs of petition : discretion of court.—45 & 46 Vict. c. 50, s. 98. 47 & 48 Vict. c. 70 (1), s. 38, sch. 2.

Power to order payment of costs by borough or by individual engaged in corrupt practices.—47 & 48 Vict. c. 70 (1), ss. 29, 32.

Accommodation for court, &c., shorthand notes of evidence.—45 & 46 Vict. c. 50, s. 99.

Rules of procedure and jurisdiction of High Court.— 45 & 46 Vict c. 50, s. 100.

Acts done pending petition not invalidated.—45 & 46 Vict. c. 50, s. 102.

New election in room of person unseated.—45 & 46 Vict. c. 50, s. 103.

No disclosure of vote in proceedings on petition.— 45 & 46 Vict. c. 50, s. 104.

Persons guilty of corrupt or illegal practices, or illegal employment, &c. ; prohibited from voting, and their votes void.—(U.K.) 46 & 47 Vict. c. 51 (1), ss. 6, 10. 37, 64. 47 & 48 Vict. c. 70 (1), s. 22.

Application to municipal elections of ss. 37 and 38 of Corrupt Practices Act, 1883.—46 & 47 Vict. c. 51 (1), s. 38 (10). 47 & 48 Vict. c. 70 (1), s. 23.

List of persons incapable of voting by reason of corrupt or illegal practices ; revision and publication thereof. —47 & 48 Vict. c. 70 (1), s. 24.

Prosecution of persons guilty of corrupt or illegal practices before election, or other court.—47 & 48 Vict. c. 70 (1). ss. 28, 30.

Director of public prosecutions, duties of, as to trial of petition, and prosecution of offenders.—47 & 48 Vict. c. 70 (1), ss. 26, (5), 28, 30.

Application of enactments to City of London municipal elections.—47 & 48 Vict. c. 70 (1), s. 35.

Application of enactments to local board and other elections.—47 & 48 Vict c. 70 (1), ss. 36, 37, sch. 1.

WATERLOW & SONS LIMITED,

List of FORMS, BOOKS, &c.,

REQUIRED BY

Presiding & Returning Officers, Candidates & Election Agents.

*These Forms have been settled by H. Stephen, Esq., and H. E. Miller, Esq.,
Barristers-at-Law. Authors of the " County Council Compendium."*

1.	Appointment of Deputy Returning Officer	1 - per dozen.
2.	Writ to Mayor of Borough to elect County Councillor, parchment	1/- each.
2a.	Writ do. do. do. when divided into Wards ...	1/- ,,
3.	Notice of Election, Poster	7/6 per 100.
4.	Nomination Form	1/6 per dozen.
5.	Suggestions for filling up Nomination Papers ...	1/- ,,
6.	Notice of Nomination, Poster	7/6 per 100.
7.	Notice of Objection to Nomination	1/- per dozen.
8.	Notice of Poll and Polling Districts, Poster ...	7/6 per 100.
9.	Appointment of Presiding Officer, Polling Clerks, &c.	1/6 per dozen.
10.	Appointment of Election Agent	1/- ,,
11.	Notification of appointment of Election Agent ...	1/- ,,
12.	Form of Appointment of Sub-Agents	1/- ,,
13.	Instructions to Sub-Agents	2/- ,,
14.	Notification to Returning Officer of appointment of Sub-Agents	1/6 ,,
15.	Form of Hire of Committee Rooms	1/- ,,
16.	Instructions for Presiding Officers, Poll Clerks, &c. ...	1/6 ,,
17.	Instructions to Agents attending Polling Stations ...	2/6 ,,
18.	Notice of Counting Votes	1/- ,,
19.	Appointment of Agent for Counting Votes ...	1/6 ,,
20.	Notification to Returning Officer of appointment of Agents for Counting Votes	2/- ,,
21.	Appointment of Agents to detect personation ...	1/6 ,,
22.	Notification to Returning Officer of appointment of same	2/- ,,
23.	Return of person elected	1/6 ,,
24.	Notice to Candidate of his Election	1/- ,,
25.	Declaration on acceptance of office	1/6 ,,
26.	Declaration of Secrecy	1/6 ,,
27.	Questions to be put	2/- ,,
28.	Declaration of inability to read	1/6 ,,
29.	List of Tendered Votes	1/6 ,,
30.	List of Votes marked by the Presiding Officer ...	1/6 ,,
31.	Admission Card to Polling Stations	5/- per 100.
32.	Form of Card to be used in Counting Ballot Papers ...	6/- ,,
33.	Declaration of Expenses	1/6 per dozen.
34.	Notice of allotment of Polling Stations, Poster ...	7/6 per 100.
35.	Notice of Situation of Polling Stations and guidance for Voting, Poster	7/6 ,,
36.	Notice of Election of Councillors unopposed, Poster ...	7/6 ,,
37.	Returning Officer's Notice of Election after contest, Poster	7/6 ,,
38.	Caution to Electors as to Corrupt Practices, Poster ...	7/6 ,,
39.	Caution to Electors as to Offences against the Ballot Act, Poster	7/6 ,,
40.	Caution as to disturbance in Polling Stations, Poster ...	7/6 ,,
41.	Ballot Papers, in books with counterpart, numbered and with Candidates' Names, *at a few hours' notice*	To order.
42.	Direction Slips, " Way In " " Way Out," Gummed Paper or Index Hands	,,
43.	Order Book	2/6 each.
44.	Notice of Polling Place	To order.

**These Forms and Books are kept in Stock, and sent off immediately
on receipt of Order.**

WATERLOW & SONS LIMITED,

LIST OF STATIONERY, &c.,

FOR POLLING STATIONS.

In Packets. Price 5/6 each, or £3 per doz.

Four large Envelopes endorsed for Papers, Books, viz. :—
1. The Unused and Spoilt Ballot Papers.
2. The Tendered Ballot Papers.
3. The Marked Copies of the Register of Voters, and the Counterfoils of the Ballot Papers.
4. The Tendered Votes List and the List of Votes marked by Presiding Officer.

Tape for fastening Up Ballot Box

Sealing Wax.
Eight Indelible Pencils for use of Voters.
Six Sheets of Blotting Paper.
Six Sheets Large Brown Paper.
Twelve Sheets Note Paper and Envelopes.
Six Pencils, Six Penholders and Pens.
One Bottle of Ink and Inkstand.
One Ball of Twine.
One Pentateuch.
One New Testament.

THE ELECTION AGENT'S CASH BOOK

(*COPYRIGHT*),

Ruled and Printed with Headings, suitable for every description of outlay, with a Summary at end of every 16 pages, enabling the Election Agent to ascertain at a glance the Expenditure incurred up to any given time.

(A) **54 leaves, super-royal 4to, bound limp roan and lettered** **12/6**

(B) **72 ditto   ditto   ditto**   ...   **16/-**

A large number of these Books were used at the last General Election, and gave great satisfaction.

LONDON WALL, LONDON.

WATERLOW & SONS LIMITED,

COUNTY COUNCIL COMPENDIUM.

OPINIONS OF THE PRESS.

"LAW TIMES" says :—"Among the expositions of the general effect of the new legislation it stands high for clearness of thought and expression. It is a well-conceived an l well-arranged piece of timely work. The Index appears comprehensive and excellent, and reflects great credit on its compiler."

"SOLICITORS' JOURNAL" says:—"The first chapter contains a terse and well-digested summary of the leading changes effected by the Act. The authors then proceed to deal with the constitution and election of county councils. The information under this head is full and clearly arranged under sub-headings."

"SATURDAY REVIEW" says :—"A lucid and able digest of the County Electors Act, the Local Government Act, and the Municipal Corporations Act, 1882. The book in fact is a concise treatise on the enormous changes in local government that will come into operation in April, and a handy volume of reference for officials and electors. The magnitude of the new scheme of Local Government is unfolded with admirable clearness and cumulative effect."

"DAILY NEWS" says :—"A complete and useful treatise upon the Local Government Acts."

"THE FIELD" says :—"THE LOCAL GOVERNMENT ACT.—The County Council Compendium must be mentioned as one of the most valuable of the books which have appeared on this subject. By the competent hands of the editor of the ninth edition of 'Stephen's Commentaries' and of Mr. Horace Miller, a clear and instructive digest has been made of the various statutes enumerated, and the effect of the recent changes is well elucidated in a preliminary chapter. There are copious notes and appendices with a full index, and numerous extracts from parliamentary papers bearing on the general subject of local government will be found included in the volume."

LONDON WALL, LONDON.

WATERLOW & SONS LIMITED,

THE LAW RELATING TO CORRUPT PRACTICES AT PARLIAMENTARY, MUNICIPAL AND OTHER ELECTIONS, AND THE PRACTICE ON ELECTION PETITIONS, with an Appendix of Statutes, Rules and Forms. By MILES WALKER MATTINSON and STUART CUNNINGHAM MACASKIE, of Gray's Inn, Barrister-at-Law. Second Edition. Demy 8vo. In cloth, 10s.

TABLE OF CORRUPT AND ILLEGAL PRACTICES WHICH VITIATE THE ELECTION. An Extract from the above work. By M. W. MATTINSON and S. C. MACASKIE, Barristers-at-Law. On linen-lined card. Prices: 1 copy, 2d.; 50 copies, 6s.; 100 copies, 10s.; 250 copies, £1 2s. 6d.; 500 copies, £2; 1,000 copies, £3 15s.

TABLE OF CORRUPT AND ILLEGAL PRACTICES WHICH VITIATE THE ELECTION, printed on stout cardboard 11 by 17, suitable for affixing to the walls of committee rooms. Price 6d. each.

A HANDBOOK OF THE LAW RELATING TO THE MANAGEMENT OF PARLIAMENTARY, COUNTY COUNCIL AND MUNICIPAL ELECTIONS. Second Edition. A statement of the Law relating to the machinery of Elections. By HENRY STEPHEN, Esq., of the Middle Temple, Barrister-at-Law. In cloth, 1s.

THE FRANCHISE ACTS, 1884-5, being the Representation of the People Act, 1884: Registration Act, 1885; and Parliamentary Elections (Redistribution) Act, 1884; with introductions and Notes. By MILES WALKER MATTINSON, Barrister-at-Law. Joint Author of "Mattinson and Macaskie on Corrupt Practices." In boards, 2s. 6d.

THE ELECTORAL BOUNDARIES OF THE UNITED KINGDOM, being Schedules 5, 6, and 7 of the Parliamentary Elections (Redistribution) Act, 1885. With Index. In boards, 2s. 6d.

LONDON WALL, LONDON.

WATERLOW & SONS LIMITED,

Opinions of the Press

ON THE WORK BY

MESSRS. MATTINSON & MACASKIE,

ON

"The Law Relating to Corrupt Practices."

"Invaluable to Electioneerers and Party Agents. . . . We "recommend it not only to every Election Agent but to every "Candidate."—WHITEHALL REVIEW.

"The difficult topic of Agency in particular is fully and clearly "treated. . . . The greater scope and careful workmanship of "this book make any comparison with other books yet published out "of the question."—LAW TIMES.

"It is compiled upon an easy intelligible plan, and has evidently "been very carefully prepared. . . . An invaluable guide to the "Statutory standard of Parliamentary probity."—GLOBE.

"A complete guide to the Election Law, and written with such a "masterful grasp of the subject and lucidity rarely to be found in "law books."—WEDNESBURY HERALD.

"Gentlemen about to embark in the adventures of Electioneering "had better get this book promptly and study it carefully."—WESTERN TIMES.

"A valuable *résumé* of the law under which future Elections will "have to be conducted."—DAILY CHRONICLE.

"A valuable, explicit, and carefully compiled compendium of "Election Law."—TOWER HAMLETS INDEPENDENT.

"To Agents and Candidates the information will be specially "valuable, for the writers point out, especially in the matter of the "use of conveyances and of the hire of Committee Rooms, not only "what is forbidden, but what is permissable."—BRIGHTON DAILY POST.

"It is of the most complete and explanatory character."—CORNISHMAN.

LONDON WALL, LONDON.

WATERLOW & SONS LIMITED,

BALLOT BOXES.

These Boxes are made of Japanned Metal with Handles and Tumbler Locks. Three Seals are placed on the front, and one with slit and slide cover on the top, for sealing up, thus effectually preventing any tampering with the contents, or the introduction or withdrawal of papers after the seals are affixed.

JAPANNED METAL—	Each.	Doz.
To take 500 Voting Papers	10/6	£6
To take 1,000 ditto	16 6	£9

PERCUSSION PRESS.

Fitted with a word of 3 or 4 letters, embossing the Paper on both sides.
7 - each.   £4 per doz.

LEVER PRESS.

A strong powerful Press. Fitted with a word of 3 or 4 letters, or a design.

9 - each.   £5. 5/- per doz.

DUPLEX PRESS.

A slight pressure on the handle produces a coloured impression on both sides of the paper. Fitted with an ordinary word of 3 or 4 letters, or a design.

10 - each.   £5. 8 - per doz.

PERFORATING PRESS.

This is the best and most effectual press for cancelling Voting Papers. Fitted with a word of 3 or 4 letters, or a design of between 50 and 60 pinholes.

10/- each.   £5. 10/- per doz.

Any of the above altered for future Elections at a charge of from 3 - each.

LONDON WALL, LONDON.